Race for Life

Race for Life

The Joel Sonnenberg Story

Janet Sonnenberg

Zondervan Publishing House
of The Zondervan Corporation
Grand Rapids, Michigan

RACE FOR LIFE
© 1983 by Janet Sonnenberg

LIBRARY OF CONGRESS CATALOGING IN PUBLICATION DATA
Sonnenberg, Janet.
  Race for life.
  1. Sonnenberg, Joel. 2. Burns and scalds—Patients—United States—
Biography. 2. Physically handicapped—United States—Biography.
I. Title.
RD96.4.S55 1983   362.4'3'0924   [B]   83-12409
ISBN 0-310-25930-4

Designed by Ann Cherryman
Edited by Judith E. Markham
Printed in the United States of America

83 84 85 86 87 88 — 10 9 8 7 6 5 4 3 2

7063192

Contents

Because I am writing Joel's story, I must tell it from my viewpoint as Joel's mother. However, I in no way have ever run this race alone. As every race has its encouraging spectators, so, too, did our race. Not only were immediate family members, friends, and medical personnel involved deeply, but many people across the country and around the world. Thus, I have interspersed sections throughout my narrative, in which from a third person viewpoint I tell what was happening to those around and beyond me.

In some instances names have been omitted or changed to protect the privacy of individuals or institutions.

Preface

I get excited when I describe Joel, our son. He dashes around the house chasing his sister Jami. His eyes twinkle with mischief. His mouth puckers in a pout. His teeth gleem when he smiles. His legs, agile and strong, move swiftly and surely as he races in our yard. He squeals with delight. He screams in anger. He exudes enthusiasm and three-year-old determination. He shoves his hands in his pockets or crosses his arms in defiance. Snuggling into my side, he whispers, "I love you, Mommie." He bounces playfully on his daddy's knee. Drawing and painting, trucks, cars, and motorcycles are his loves. Bear hugs are his specialty. He is a bundle of promise and potential.

Yet if you were to see our son in a grocery store, shopping with his mother as children do, you would probably stare in disbelief or look away hastily. For Joel is severely and permanently facially disfigured. And if you stayed to watch this courageous child handle some canned goods or carry a bag of potato chips to the grocery cart, you would be further startled to realize that he lacks one hand and has no fingers on the other.

But it wasn't always so. Once Joel was a beautiful, blond-haired baby boy.

On September 15, 1979, my husband Mike and I, with our children Jami and Joel, were headed for the southern Maine coast for a weekend retreat after a long summer of hard work. With us were Mike's sister and her husband, Kathy and Doug Rupp. They had driven all night from Ohio to begin their New England vacation with us.

The beach awaited us—surf and seagulls stirred in our imagination as we headed out early that Saturday morning. I could already see the children running up and down the beach, cool Maine air tossing their hair, their bodies exhausted after full days of outdoor fun.

We never got to Maine. And instead of running for fun up and down the beach, we found ourselves running for survival in a great race—against immense odds. Now, as we press on to enhance the promise and potential of a full life for Joel, we are still running. This is the story.

Mother's Day, 1981

The Race
for
Survival

Saturday, September 15, 1979

The asphalt vibrated. The earth seemed to shake as the immense tractor-trailer bore down on us. The rest area where we had pulled off the interstate seemed a perfect place for the children to run, and we could all stretch and relax before the fifty remaining miles to Maine. Delighted to give their legs a workout, Jami and Joel ran along the roadside. Suddenly we heard the deafening roar of a powerhouse engine as the immense semi streaked toward us. My muscles iced. Where were the children? I saw our three-year-old Jami safe on the other side of the car and screamed, "Mike, where's Joel?" But the truck was right beside us now. My question was muffled by the suction and storm of diesel-filled air. Sudden silence. The ghostly truck had vanished down the highway as quickly as it had appeared.

"I've got him," Mike called, his arms wrapped tightly around Joel. Then he added, "Let's switch cars." The kids needed a change of scenery, and the switch might alleviate some of the impatience we were all feeling in our desire to reach Maine. So Mike, Doug, and Joel piled into the front seat of our large, aging green Chevy, while Kathy, Jami, and myself rode in luxury in the Rupp's new Mercury.

"Vacation," I sighed to myself, settling back into the soft glove-leather seat. "This has to be a special retreat. Everything is so right." It was just a short weekend trip to Maine, but that didn't dim my enthusiasm for this first vacation our family had ever taken. Noticing the bright, crisp skies and abundant sunshine, I gloated, "We've picked a winner for our first taste of autumn." As we traveled, Jami had been scanning the fleeting woods for splashes of color, signaling birthday season at our house, while colors had held Joel's interest only if they were in the form of trucks. We had all day to make a half-day trip. No wash to do, no dishes, no time schedule to keep, no phone to ring or checkbook to balance. Ahhh—this must be a vacation!

Kathy slowed down for the tollbooth two miles past the rest area where we had stopped. Tuning back into reality I gazed intently into the car in front of us where Joel sat sandwiched between Mike and Doug. I could see his little blond head bobbing back and forth above the infant seat.

"Joel is having such a good time," I thought, as Kathy and I talked about her new job in Ohio as a car saleswoman. Bursting air brakes interrupted our chatter. Ahead of us I saw Mike, his arm outstretched, paying the toll. Turning toward the sound I glimpsed the grill of a tractor-trailer bearing down on us. Then the tremendous force of thirty-six tons of metal thrust us forward. Time seemed suspended. Silence enveloped me as my body, trapped in and protected by a molded skeleton of steel, tossed in response to the impact. An accident!

"Can this be happening?" I asked as my body seemed to be in slow-motion. I fell sideways and I heard the truck at my window. Glass pulverized about me.

"Lord, here I come to You." I expected every bone to be crushed by the steel monster. At that moment, I felt peaceful—as if the Lord and I were in the same house, but He was in another room. I felt ready to walk into His room, and I was just telling Him I was coming.

My head hit the back of the seat as it seemed we hit a wall of concrete. There was another jolt at the rear of the car and the thought, "What about Jami?" flooded my mind with fear as my forehead grazed the dashboard. Dead silence. It was over. I was exhausted. My head felt heavy. I wanted to sleep.

Forcing myself awake, I yelled, "Jami?" and turned in relief as I heard her crying. She wasn't unconscious. She looked okay.

Then, out of the corner of my eye I saw smoke and flame outside the car, seemingly coming from the rear bumper. Fire! Adrenaline surged into my blood stream. The car was going to explode! Were we trapped inside?

I noticed with relief that all the glass was out of the windows. We could crawl out if we had to. I tried frantically to open my door. It wouldn't budge.

"Get out! Get out as fast as you can!" I urged Kathy. She opened her door with much effort. It seemed to take us forever to get out.

With Jami clutching at my neck and her legs wrapped around my waist, we ran as fast as we could away from the car and away from the truck beside us.

"It's going to blow! It's going to blow!" I screamed as we ran in terror. I curled my toes in to allow my shoes to grip tighter so I could run faster. I couldn't see where I was going, stumbled, and almost fell with Jami in my arms. We finally rounded the corner of the tollbooth away from the truck, panting, hearts pounding.

We had escaped! It didn't seem possible, but we had! Suddenly, Kathy cried, "Where are the guys?"

Never once had it occurred to me that my husband, son, and brother-in-law had also been hit by the truck and with much greater impact.

"Look!" Kathy screamed and pointed behind us. I could vaguely make out a car, totally engulfed in flames. A green Chevy! Ours!

The truck had rammed a total of five cars, lined up at the tollbooth. The impact had pushed Kathy's car, the third vehicle to be hit, into our Chevy and then onto the top of the concrete abutment sheltering the tollbooth. Then the truck rammed our Chevy with its final, full impact.

"They're gone!" Kathy and I moaned, our arms around each other, too terrified to move toward the flames, to see our husbands' bodies trapped in the wreckage. Suddenly a large man loomed toward us, covered in soot, clothes ripped, shreds of material dangling from his arms.

"Surely this must be the truck driver," I reasoned silently, backing away in terror. "Jan, it's Mike!" cried Kathy. I looked again.

"Mike!" I screamed in relief. "Where's Joel?" The question filled every muscle and every nerve with terror. With glazed eyes, Mike moaned, "He was such a neat son."

"My baby! My baby!" I screamed in disbelief and horror. Where was my baby? His face flashed in front of me, the long, dark eyelashes, the plump, kissable cheeks, his precious smile and soft blond hair. A dull thud sounded in the recesses of my mind.

"Jan," Kathy's voice sounded an awesome warning. "It's Joel."

She was looking behind her at something on the ground. I turned and saw a small body, smoldering, totally black, charred beyond recognition, lying in an infant seat.

"Joel?" I asked. I handed Jami to Kathy and bent down for a closer look. Holding my breath in disbelief, kneeling on the grass along the interstate, I fully took in the sight before me. The child's face was black. The hair was gone, and the top of the head was white. The eyelids were burned shut, charred and beginning to swell. The nose was black and shrunken. The lips were burned off, and what was left was puffy but also contracted. The blackened arms, crisp with carbon, were outstretched and quivering.

I grabbed one of the arms as a point of contact, only to withdraw quickly; the arm was so hot I couldn't even touch it. Then the clothes shocked me into reality. The denim bib overalls, the brand-name label still hanging on the front pocket, and the low-topped baby shoes screamed at me. It *was* Joel! I had dressed him in these clothes this morning!

"Joel, Joel—Joel," I moaned with greater intensity every time I said it. I moaned his name over and over. It couldn't be! It had to be—I recognized the clothes. It was. It *was* Joel.

"Joel!" I screamed, gripped by agony for my son and myself.

As I sobbed, I wanted to yell, "Why was he saved?" Sudden anger filled me. "Why was he saved? He's going to die. He's going to die."

As a nurse, I could not doubt in those moments that my baby was, indeed, going to die. Every piece of his body visible to me seemed burned. I had been taught that few survive such massive burns. As a mother, I could see no reason for Joel to be saved from the burned wreckage only to suffer horribly and die anyway. What torture! What waste! More anger filled me! Just a few more seconds and he would have been at peace.

Suddenly a young man grabbed my arm. "Lady, I saved your baby! I saved your baby!" he breathlessly implored. He groaned as he said it and held his hands strangely.

"He's going to be all right. He's going to be all right!" he tried to convince me.

I wanted to scream back, "You jerk! Why did you save him? He's going to die. You don't know what you're talking about!"

Instead, I said a quiet "Thank you" between sobs. But the absurdity of the man's statement interrupting my thoughts and my grief seemed to switch me to a new channel. I began to ask, "What can I do for Joel? What can I do, as a nurse, for my son?"

Another question came, sure and strong, "Is he breathing?" I stopped sobbing abruptly, my own breath coming in short spurts now as I wiped away the tears with my hands to see better. I honestly couldn't tell if he was breathing or not. His chest didn't seem to be moving.

As I leaned over him, the stench of my son's burnt body overpowered me. Did I feel air coming from his nose or mouth onto my cheek? No. The acrid smoke was repulsive as I forced a quick spurt of my own air into his lipless, contracted mouth. He choked as if inhaling smoke. I backed off.

Then Joel started screaming, his whole body quivering—the sound filled my body and my mind. He screamed and screamed. His voice filled the air around me. It seemed to pierce my bones. He kept screaming in his terrified pain. What should I do now?

"At least he's breathing," I reasoned to stop the panic rising inside me.

An ambulance attendant had arrived now and poured a pitcher of cold water on Joel's torso. As I saw the steam rising from the water contacting Joel's hot body, my first reaction was, "Won't the steam burn him worse?" But a doctor who came running to us from the traffic backed up on the interstate ordered the ambulance attendant to keep pouring the water (in order to cool down Joel's body and stop the progressive damage inflicted by the heat).

Joel kept screaming. I couldn't think of Joel's pain—I just couldn't handle that—but I could try to comfort him. I knew he was scared; he couldn't see or understand what was happening to him. And I knew that he might be able to hear me. So I kept repeating, "Mommie's here, Joel. Mommie's here," sobbing as I said it, for I felt so helpless.

Then I looked at his feet. The leather baby shoes were partially burned and Joel's ankles looked puffy.

"These shoes will cut off his circulation," I thought as I tried to pull them off. But they wouldn't budge. Next I undid the metal buckles on the straps of his bib overalls; they were so hot that I was frantic to get them away from his skin. I decided to keep him in the infant seat since it held him semi-upright, a good position for breathing. (Little did I know that later the nurses and doctors in the emergency room would have to pull with all their might to get him out. The plastic had melted into his body, and as it cooled, it fused into his burned tissues.)

I wasn't aware that Mike was beside me, his arm around me for comfort. The shock of looking at Joel jolted Mike into full consciousness of his own pain, for Mike, too, was injured.

Kathy cried, "Jan, Mike's hurt!" A nurse and ambulance attendant had noticed that Mike was oozing blood from the back of his head. It was dripping down his neck onto the ground and into my hair as he held me. They forced Mike to sit down on the ground as they attended to him. I looked over—he didn't look too bad to me. He *couldn't* be badly hurt. I wouldn't *let* him be hurt. I had to dismiss Mike's injury from my mind. "Doug's hurt, too. He's over against the building." But I couldn't think about anyone but Joel.

Ambulances arrived. I never heard their sirens. A young man bent over Joel and said to me, "Let's lift him into the back of the ambulance." Using the charred infant seat as a stretcher, we lifted Joel and ran to the ambulance. During the momentum of running, I began to realize that we were running for Joel's survival. Indeed, it began to seem that the promise of his life *was* worth struggling for—the race against death *was* a race worth running.

Again, I asked myself, "What can I do for Joel?" But the ambulance attendants wanted me to sit in the cab of the ambulance. In the enclosed vehicle, Joel's screaming seemed to intensify.

"Give him some O$_2$," I yelled to the people in the back.

"Just shut up, lady," the driver said. "You just sit there and be quiet. I don't want to hear one word out of you!" His voice was angry and nervous. He was so shaken up I wondered how he would ever get us to the hospital!

The siren started wailing as we drove down the interstate. In the back, they were having trouble getting the oxygen started. The doctor comforted the attendant, "Don't worry—this kid's not going to make it anyway."

But in the cab, I was concentrating on Joel's survival. We were going to a hospital, but where? How far was it? I didn't even know where we were.

"How far is it to the hospital?" I timidly asked the driver.

"Fifteen to twenty minutes," came the terse reply as he leaned forward in the seat intent on his driving.

"So far to go," I thought as we made a few turns and crossed a bridge. "We must get there quickly. It must be a little hospital. I wonder if they'll know what they're doing?"

Joel's face flashed in front of me again. His long, dark eyelashes, the tufts of blond hair on the top of his head, his sweet face. I remembered sitting in a booth with the kids at McDonald's the day before. Joel was jumping up and down on the seat, flirting with the elderly ladies in the booth next to us, smiling and throwing them kisses. They were enamored with him, and I was proud he was my son. I remembered walking out thinking about what a great day it was as Joel and Jami skipped along beside me. I remembered wishing we could always be as happy as we were at that very moment.

I came back to reality. Joel had been burned—what could I do? Suddenly, a whole new scene flashed in front of me. I was sitting in a classroom with my fellow nursing students and the nursing instructor was lecturing on burns. Burns were an awful injury to care for. Dressing changes were so involved they took hours: layers of gauze wrapped round and round the wounds; creams put on and scrubbed off. The layers of gowns, gloves, and masks needed for sterility were cumbersome. The patients were demanding; their pain was intense.

This nursing instructor had had a strong personality and commanded attention. Her voice came back to me now above the roar of the siren. To understand what happens when a body is burned, think of cooking an egg. The egg white, the protein, becomes congealed, not just in the muscle and tissue outside the bloodstream but within the blood itself. This lowers the cellular protein level. And what happens when this occurs? The fluid—water and electrolytes—shifts away from the blood and into the tissues. This is why a burn victim swells. You must replace this fluid as quickly as possible without overloading, that is, without giving your patient too much fluid. The urine output of your patient will be your index of how much fluid to put in. At first the person will put out very little, if any, urine at all because the kidneys are hoarding the fluid needed for the body to sustain life. Urine output must be established or the toxinous poisons the body produces build up in the bloodstream, causing certain death.

My mind flipped back as we approached the hospital. It wasn't as small as it could be, I noticed with relief.

Since Joel's care was out of my hands right now, my most vital link with help seemed to be the telephone. The first number that came to mind was my friend, Bev, back home in Nyack, New York, and with it the reality of our community prayer chain and its power. "Bev, we've been in a very bad car accident. Joel is so badly burned. He's burned all over and he probably won't live. Mike's been hurt, he's got a burned hand, but he's going to be okay and so is everyone else."

I asked her to start prayer for Joel right away. It seemed the power of prayer was the only thing that could possibly keep Joel alive. In the span of time which bridged my kneeling down beside my burned son by the roadside and making the phone calls in the sterile hospital environment, I began to have hope.

Next I called Mike's mother in Boca Raton, Florida. I knew a vast network existed in the Christian community in the southern part of that state, and I knew Mike's mother to be a great prayer warrior and that she could contact many family members and friends.

It never occurred to me to contact these people just to let them know about our accident. It was the power of prayer I was after. I knew it was there and that it had to be harnessed for Joel. It had to be directed and channeled for my son. Joel and I were in a great race, it seemed. Soon it would be clear that we weren't alone, but in those moments it was just the two of us in a great battle against odds. But what we needed most was to move the hands of God.

In the emergency room of the small southern New Hampshire hospital a young pediatrician and a middle-aged general practitioner desperately leafed through medical books to determine what should be done for this badly burned child who needed immediate medical intervention. Both were well-trained, talented doctors, but neither had seen a case so severe before.

They did not expect the child to live, but knew if there was any chance, it was in Boston. But he must be taken there quickly.

The pediatrician approached me as I stepped from the telephone booth.

"We are transferring your son to Boston as soon as possible," he explained. "I don't think I have to explain to you the seriousness of his injury since you are a nurse—"

"I know. Thank you for your help," I replied. Kathy was waiting in the hallway. And my Jami—I threw my arms around her, stroked her ruffled, thick, brown hair and gazed into her deep brown eyes rimmed with thick lashes. My poor little girl, three years old, soon-to-be four. She had seen so much horror in the last thirty minutes. She was crying for her blanket, now ashes in the trunk of the car. Her world was crashing in and she wanted something to hang onto; Mommie, flitting from the telephone to the nurses, hadn't had time for her until that moment.

As I hugged Jami, Kathy and I discussed what to do. We had no clothes. They, too, were ashes in the car. We had no money. Where was Mike? How was he? What about Jami? Was she really all right? What about Doug? I felt I should go to Boston with Joel since he was so critically injured, but what about Jami and Kathy? Where would they stay?

A tall, blonde woman in her late thirties, neatly dressed, came forward. She explained that she was Nancy MacKenzie, a lab technologist at the hospital. She had overheard us and wanted to be of help.

"You can come and stay at my house," she offered Kathy and reassured me, "I'll take care of your little girl." There was concern in her soft voice and in her kind eyes. I had no reason to doubt her competence and liked her instantly, trusted her. Kathy, with Nancy's help, would take good care of my Jami.

"Jami, I love you very much." I hugged her to my chest, stroked her hair again, and spoke to her softly. "Joel is hurt badly, honey, and Mommy is going to a bigger hospital in another town to take care of him. I'll call you on the phone every day. Aunt Kathy will take care of you. Daddy will be here, too, and you'll get to talk to him on the telephone and maybe visit him while he's in the hospital. I love you very much. Never forget, Jesus is always with you."

As I walked away from my daughter to find Mike, I thought, "Thank God Jami wasn't injured! Thank God most of us have survived this holocaust." I wanted to pinch my arm to make sure I was alive. It still seemed unreal—less than an hour before I had expected to be walking into the next room to meet the Lord in heaven, and here I was wandering around in a hospital!

I was directed to a little curtained-off room in the emergency area where a doctor and two nurses were working efficiently. They were shaving the back of Mike's head in preparation for stitches while Mike kept moaning, "Get me some ice water for my hand. Get me some ice water." They were giving Mike injections to numb the areas the doctor needed to stitch. Mike was shaking from shock. Thankfulness welled up inside me—he was alive.

"Honey, how are you?"

"Oh, I'm still alive and kicking," Mike joked.

I knew he was in awful pain. His face was swelling and his

hand was gruesome whitish purple. He saw me staring at it and rasped, "My hand is burned bad." Someone was cutting off the wedding ring I had given him eight years before. His whole body quivered as the doctor asked him to turn on his side.

"Honey, they are transfering Joel to Boston."

"Go with him—be with him," Mike urged, still trying to turn over for the doctor.

"They don't think he's going to live," I explained, crying.

"I know. He was the neatest kid," Mike went on. "We were so lucky to have him for two years. He had the neatest personality— he was so much fun." We cried together and hugged each other.

"Honey, I can't believe we weren't killed. I can't believe we're alive!" I said.

"How's Jami?" Mike asked.

"She's fine, honey. Kathy's taking care of her."

"Let's pray together," Mike implored and began, "Thank You, Lord, for Joel. Thank You for giving him to us. He was so neat. He was a gift. We thank You for every day that You gave him into our care. We ask, O Lord, Your will be done with his life. Thank You for saving the rest of us from this accident. Amen."

"There's a phone call for you, Mrs. Sonnenberg," the nurse interrupted. I wondered who could be calling me in the emergency room.

"Jan, how's Joel? How are you? What happened?" It was Barb, my friend and neighbor. Bev had called her with the news.

"Barb, it was a real bad accident. Joel is terribly burned. They don't think he's going to live." I started to cry.

Barb was crying, too. "Jan, what can we do? What can any of us do to help you?"

Her question threw me. I didn't know.

"Can we come up there and get Jami and bring her back here to stay with us?"

No. I thought. *Jami has a place to stay here where she'll at least be close to Mike.* So I told Barb, "Perhaps in a little while, but for right now she is being taken care of by Kathy and a woman here at the hospital who is going to take both of them to her house."

She asked about Mike and I told her what I knew about the extent of his injuries. But I couldn't ask her for help because I honestly didn't know what to request.

"Mrs. Sonnenberg, the ambulance is leaving for Boston."

I handed the phone to Kathy and rushed out into the waiting room, only to find that the ambulance had already left! Joel had begun his journey to Boston and I was not with him!

An off-duty nurse had been called and asked if she would be able to go in attendance to help transport a child to Boston.

Yes, she could.

When she arrived at the hospital and saw the child on the stretcher in the ambulance, she could not believe her eyes. He kept screaming and screaming.

Suddenly, half-way to Boston, he ceased crying. Petrified, not knowing what to do next, the nurse poured one of the bottles of intravenous solution over his torso to stimulate his breathing. It worked. The screaming continued strong and sure as they pulled up to a Boston medical center an hour later.

Back in New Hampshire, the nurse in charge of the emergency room that evening quit her job and went to work in a doctor's office. She never again wanted to see the sights she had seen that day.

A fireman approached me in the waiting room and poured coins into my pocket. "Here's some change for your phone calls. You're going to need it."

"How am I going to get to Boston?" I implored. "The ambulance just left without me."

"I'll take you when I get off work at 6:00 P.M.," he said immediately. "I'll call my wife and have her pick you up here in forty-five minutes. She'll bring you over to the station house, and we'll leave together from there."

I barely grasped these details. All the complications seemed too much to digest. Too many feelings and questions were bombarding me. . . .

There were more papers to sign now. I tried to read them carefully, for I knew these papers were important legal documents to allow for treatment of my husband and perhaps my daughter. But I was distracted, anxious about signing so many without the time or concentration to do so with confidence, afraid of making a mistake.

Nancy MacKenzie thrust a twenty-dollar bill in my hand as she walked me out to where the fireman's wife was waiting in her car. "You're going to need this," she said.

The need for money hadn't crossed my mind at all. I was like a robot, concentrating only on getting to Boston and being at my son's side. I never asked, "Where I will I stay?" "What will I wear?" or "What will I eat?" As it turned out, I didn't need to give these questions one bit of my energy.

Nancy continued to reassure me. "Don't worry about your Jami. We are a family who loves the Lord. We'll take good care of her. And remember Romans 8:28, '*All* things work together for good to them who love God.' "

Joel's charred, rigid body flashed into my mind; the stench of his burned body still lingered on my clothes. I wanted to hit Nancy squarely between the eyes for quoting this verse to me. Such an easy thing to say! Such a glib, pat Christian slogan!

But this Bible verse, familiar to me since childhood, was to haunt me for a long time. How could this promise of God be true for us? For Joel? How could this whole mess be "good"? As these questions surfaced in my mind now, I pushed them back down. I needed to concentrate on the race for Joel's survival.

Crawling into the back seat of the fireman's car, I felt confined and vulnerable. It was a sports car, small compared to our large Chevy which now lay smashed and burned somewhere. As we drove off, cars seemed to loom at me, and I relived the impact of the accident. *If we had been traveling in this car an hour ago, we'd all be at the morgue now.* My muscles tensed; my knees shook; my voice threatened to wobble. *These people, too, are being so kind. Concentrate on that.*

"How far is it to Boston?" I asked.

"About an hour," the man replied.

That long? As the man dodged the little car in and out of traffic, I was acutely aware of all the "crazy drivers" on the road. The first tractor-trailer bearing down on us from behind almost sent me through the roof. Then I told myself, *I don't think I've been spared from this holocaust only to die on the road to Boston,* and was able to turn my attention to this kind couple, complete strangers, driving me to another strange city. Then I realized, the fireman's wife was pregnant!

"When are you due?" I asked her.

"In three weeks."

Joel, my baby, was near death; this woman was about to bring her first child into the world. For both of us, the promise of life was important.

"You know," I said, "I can't understand why this is happening. But there has to be some purpose in it. I want Joel to live so much—but a miracle seems to be the only way it could happen. I know God can do miracles." *But will He?*

"Now, if you believe in miracles, I'll tell you what'll be a miracle—" the fireman interrupted gruffly.

We were approaching the first tollbooth of our journey. I wheeled around in panic, thinking, *It'll be a miracle if we're not hit from behind again.*

"If we get to the hospital without getting lost, it'll be a miracle," he continued. I certainly could understand what he meant. Mike and I had vacationed in Boston once before our children were born, and we had marveled at the spidery web of streets, seemingly spun without rhyme or reason. Someone later told us that Boston streets were so disordered because they had once been cowpaths.

Now an amazing thing was happening. Every street we turned down was the correct route. And we pulled up in front of the medical complex without getting lost! As I walked inside the mammoth building, I began to panic again about Joel. My heart beat rapidly and my mouth became dry. It was all I could do to keep from shaking.

We asked for Joel and the receptionist pointed us in the direction of the emergency room, where again we asked, "Is Joel Sonnenberg here? The little boy badly burned?"

"They've taken him across town to another medical center."

I was surprised and upset Joel and I were still separated! And this meant another journey in the dark maze of streets. I wondered if I would ever see Joel again, alive. Couldn't a massively burned child dashing through Boston in a screaming ambulance also get lost in the maze?

Back in the cramped car, the fireman said, "Now, if you think it was a miracle we got here without getting lost, it'll be a double miracle if we get to the other medical center. I've been there many times, but never from this location!" But again, we pulled up to our destination without having to ask further directions or retrace a street. We ran inside and asked where we should go. Finally, we were near Joel.

The emergency room was bustling with activity, and the receptionist had someone lead us down a hallway away from the activity. It was very quiet. Suddenly, I remembered a day six years earlier: Mike's father had been in an automobile accident. Mike, his mother, and I were hustled into the emergency room, wondering if dad was still alive. Then we were directed away from the emergency room to a quieter area where we were told that Mike's father had died. Would history repeat itself? Would they soon be bringing me the message that my son was dead?

Our escort opened up an office. The three of us sat down, and I waited in the quiet for the tragic news, expecting the worst. When the door opened, I almost started sobbing. A nurse briskly walked in and said, "Mrs. Sonnenberg, your son is in the operating room right now. How old is he? They don't know how much anesthesia they should give him, not knowing his age."

The Race for Survival   25

"Twenty-two months," I replied, and wanted to cry, *just a baby*.
"They thought he was four, he's so large," she said as she rushed out to tell the doctors.

I sighed with relief. Joel was still alive. But what were they doing to him? What kind of operation did he need? I heard another female voice in the hallway say to the nurse who had just left, "They are so shook up in there!" to which there was the reply, "Well, many of these doctors have kids of their own, you know."

The nurse returned with papers for me to sign. She told me that the chief resident of surgery would be in soon to talk to me and asked if I needed anything to eat. The thought of food was nauseating, but her offer of a cup of coffee for myself and the fireman and his wife sounded good. I sipped the steaming liquid gratefully, its warmth soothing me.

But my stomach tightened nervously at the thought of talking with the doctor. Bracing myself for bad news, I was not prepared for the bulk of man who strode into the office. His tall frame filled the entire doorway. And he gazed down at me with the most sorrowful eyes I had ever seen on a physician.

"Mrs. Sonnenberg," he sighed, as he settled into the chair beside me, "I hear you're a nurse. We've just performed an escharotomy on your son."

"A what? I've never heard of it."

"Well, it's like bi-valving a cast," he explained. "As the burnt tissue on your son's extremities swells, it acts like a cast, or a tourniquet, cutting off the blood supply to the living, unburned tissue underneath. What we do is slit the extremities here—" he ran his fingers down his own arms in a straight line, demonstrating how they had cut into what was part of Joel's arms but now was charred and dead. I understood and nodded my head.

"He hasn't put out much urine at all, but we gave him some medicine and a little is coming out. It's very bloody, but hopefully it will be clearing up in the next twenty-four hours." Then he went on with a sigh, "Being a nurse, I don't think I have to explain to you the seriousness of your child's injuries." His eyes became darker and sadder. "This is complete devastation," he sighed heavily, shaking his head back and forth, his voice lowering. "Complete devastation." He said it slowly, rhythmically, as though convincing himself that what he had seen was real. I cried. There were tears in his eyes, too.

"What are Joel's chances?" I asked.

"Well, he's burned at least 85 percent—third degree. He probably has a 10 percent chance of surviving at the most."

"A 10 percent chance!" Adrenaline surged through me again. I had thought there was no chance at all! Ten percent was better than nothing. It was something! It wasn't *complete* devastation— Joel was breathing, wasn't he? Joel was crying, wasn't he?

With renewed boldness I said, "Doctor, I'm sure you've heard many parents say this before, but with all sincerity I want you to know that you are working on a very strong child. If there is a chance of surviving this injury, I am sure Joel can do it. Do you believe in miracles?" I asked him through tears.

"Well, I've seen the unexplainable. Yes, I guess you could say I believe in miracles."

"I just want you to know that I believe in them, and I believe a miracle can happen. I don't know if it will, but God can do a miracle for my son. I want you to know this ahead of time so that when it happens you'll know we were looking for it."

Why not expect the impossible? I only had one son—the sweetest, the cutest son—and I wanted him alive! With every breath in my body I would fight to keep him alive. Now I wanted Joel to sense this, to feel this strength. We would pull out all the stops, Joel and I. We would run this race together.

"In the next twenty-four hours your son will be going through what we call 'fluid resuscitation.' All the fluid that has shifted into the surrounding tissue we will be replenishing into his bloodstream. This is the first crisis. If he survives this, the second crisis will follow within the next several days as the fluid that has shifted into the tissues is mobilized back into the bloodstream. There is danger then of overloading the circulatory system with too much fluid."

I remembered my nursing instructor likening the blood vessels—veins, arteries, capillaries—to a set of pipes and the heart to a pump. I envisioned a small pipe being overloaded with more water than it could handle. It would finally burst open. I imagined a pump being forced to manage too much fluid. It would break down.

"We will monitor your son very closely," the doctor went on. "If he survives the second crisis, he will then be in a battle against infection. Without skin his body is open to anything in the air or in the surrounding physical environment; the invasion of germs is tremendous. This will be his biggest battle after the first days— and it will last weeks and weeks. It will be his greatest battle. He has a long fight ahead of him if he lives through these next days."

I was not dismayed at the doctor's news. In fact, I liked his futuristic thinking. Talking about Joel's future gave me hope, even if, unbelievably at this point, it meant greater struggles than what he faced now. My certainty that Joel would not survive vanished. I had a sense of promise. There was *a chance*!

"Now, what about you?" the surgeon asked as he glanced over my face. "Where is your husband?" I explained briefly that Mike had been injured and was back in New Hampshire and that we had no relatives or friends in Boston because we lived in New York. Stating the predicament made me realize my aloneness. Suddenly I felt very helpless and vulnerable.

"Don't worry," he assured me. "I'm going to assign a nurse to take care of your needs." It was a relief to know somebody was going to be available to help me.

Shortly after the surgeon left, the nurse I had talked to earlier walked in. As a nurse, I felt she was a colleague. She also had a "take charge" attitude and a caring manner I liked. At that point I needed to feel someone was in control of the situation.

"My name is Marge, and the doctor has assigned me to take care of you. I'm right here if you need me. First of all, I'm going to give you a few free phone calls. You can call anywhere and talk to anyone you want to in the United States."

I was baffled. Who should I call? Barb's caring call to me came to mind, so I decided to phone her first.

"Barb, everyone is so nice here. They give me coffee. They are giving me free phone calls—"

Barb, frightened by my calmness, interjected, "Jan, *what about Joel.*?" I started sobbing and moaning into the telephone, racked with grief and pain. Barb cried along with me. "Jan, I can't believe this has really happened to you. To *you*. I'm just heartbroken for you. I love you. I care for you."

Hearing Barb say this was comforting—someone hurt with me and cared enough to say it.

"Barb, they only give Joel a 10 percent chance of living. I want him to live so much. He's got to. I don't think I can stand it if he doesn't. You know, just last night I was holding him in my arms on the couch before I put him in his crib. Jami was on the floor and I felt torn because I wanted to give her some attention, too, but I felt like just holding Joel." I was sobbing again.

"Usually I'm so tired at the end of the day that I just put him in his crib with his bottle, but last night was different. It was like I couldn't put him down. I kept gazing on his face, so serene, so handsome and beautiful. I kissed his cheek. I stroked his hair. I thought about how terrible it would be to lose a child. I thought about how I didn't think I could live without my children—how empty my life would be without them." I started moaning with grief.

"Now listen, Jan," Barb said urgently, "I've got this feeling— you know how I get these feelings sometimes—" I just had to giggle at her comment, perhaps a bit hysterically. But it was so typical of Barb; she was always having "feelings" about things.

"Jan, listen to me!" she urged, raising her voice so I would hear her, as though at long-distance taking me by the shoulders and shaking me over and over. "You've got to listen to me! I know it's crazy, but I've got this feeling—I feel this very strongly. Joel is a very strong little boy—if anyone can make it through this, it's Joel!" She was right. I'd said the same words to the doctor, earnestly wanting him to believe me. Now I was being challenged to believe them myself.

When Jan Sonnenberg used her free phone calls to contact key friends and relatives on Saturday, September 15, 1979, a network of love and concern began. Barb was on the phone all evening after she learned about Joel's condition. She acted as a switchboard operator and messenger, contacting every person she could think of who knew the Sonnenberg family, or even people she just knew would pray.

Throughout the night and on into Sunday morning, phones were ringing in homes across the United States. And, like candles lighted in the darkness here and there across the country, people began to pray, seeking God's healing power for Joel, Mike and Doug, and God's comfort for Jan, Jami, and Kathy.

The Sonnenberg's home church in Nanuet, New York, activated its prayer chain. Other churches were notified. In Nyack, New York, the faculty, staff, and students of Nyack College where Mike was a professor of biology began to pray and to call people they knew. As the network of concern and prayer spread, more candles of faith were lighted as people responded to the news of the accident and Joel's desperate condition.

With this prayer network came a network of people ready to put their love and faith into action.

In Michigan, Janet's mother prepared to fly to Boston within the next twenty-four hours in order to be with her daughter and grandson. In Florida, Mike's mother arranged an early flight to be with her son, daughter, and granddaughter.

In Boston, Marge—the nurse who had been assigned to help—called a boardinghouse down the street from the hospital and insisted that a room be provided for Janet.

Two of Janet's friends in New York made plans to go to Boston to help. Donna Nielsen, an intensive-care nurse, knew she could help by being on hand to assist in Joel's care. Janet Krellwitz, a music professor, and her husband, Jerry, left their own month-old baby with grandparents, who had driven up from New Jersey, to head for Boston to be with Jan and Joel and give what practical help they could.

Meanwhile in New Hampshire, Mike Sonnenberg, badly burned and confined to a bed in a private room separated from his wife, his daughter, and his son, was trying to dictate lists of arrangements to be made, contingent on whether Joel lived or died.

"Mrs. Sonnenberg, we will now be going up to see your son," Marge announced. "He's in a new room that has just been refurbished with all the newest equipment so we can efficiently care for more seriously ill patients. Joel is on a respirator—not because he isn't breathing on his own, but because we don't want him wasting a lot of his energy on breathing. He needs his energy to fight his burns. Do you have any questions before we go up?"

I didn't, but after desiring to be near Joel for so many hours, I was now apprehensive. Would he look a lot different than he had at the scene of the accident?

Donning the cumbersome gown, gloves, mask, and hat—all the apparel intended to protect Joel from germs—I nervously followed Marge into his room.

Joel was naked—lying on his back, spread eagle. Mummy-like bandages enveloped his arms and legs. The mechanical inspiration-expiration rhythm of the respirator was syncopated by the ever beating blip of the heart monitor as well as the frequent alarms from the machine monitoring the intravenous fluids. I noticed that Joel had huge leg and arm splints attached to his extremities, and Marge explained that these were to keep his legs and arms straight so irreversible damage would not be caused to his muscles and ligaments from lying immobilized for a long period of time.

The two nurses in the room introduced themselves to me, but I stood back, detached from the scene. Draped in sterile garments, watching the nurses work with the machines, monitor my son's vital signs, I felt more like a nurse than a mother. I asked about Joel's vital signs almost clinically, wanting all the information I could get about his physical course. I looked at the flow chart— a record of all the physical data collected by the nurses. Every time they measured his urine, took his temperature and pulse, they recorded it on this chart. A glance at this record gave a quick overview of the physiological condition of the patient.

Patient. The word meant many different things to me. I had cared for patients before, many kinds of people with many different problems. But none of them had been my son. My son—a patient. Me, his mother—a nurse. These two roles seemed to go together because they were both vital parts of *me,* linked closely and deeply within me. Yet, each role was also different, separate.

As a nurse, I feared imcompetence. Did these nurses really know what they were doing? A mistake could be fatal to my son. As a mother, I feared that if I left the room I might never see Joel alive again. I also feared that if his condition did deteriorate, no one would tell me or let me be with my son during his last minutes.

When my friend Donna arrived in the middle of the night, her presence reassured me that I could leave the room for some much-needed sleep. As both a nurse and a friend, she would awaken me if a crisis should arise. So at 4:00 A.M., September 16, I finally fell asleep on an old cot in the room next-door to my son.

Sunday

When I awoke at 6:00 A.M., after sleeping only two hours, I sat up and looked around. Reality hit me full-force as soon as my eyes flicked open. Yes, I was in a hospital. Yes, Joel had been badly burned in that awful accident. Tears engulfed me. I cried and cried, my whole body broken with grief. I folded my arms to my chest as if hugging Joel. I imagined his little blond head, his strong body on my lap, my arms around him, holding him, protecting him from harm. I held on tight—sobbing and grieving and realizing what had happened.

Joel had been destroyed by fire. The fire! My own child sizzling in those flames I had seen leaping higher than our car. My mind fought the vivid images. A truck rear-ending a string of cars at a tollbooth? Joel, my son, torched by the gasoline from the tank of our car? The only person critically injured in the whole, awful mess had to be my Joel? My beautiful, coordinated, easy-going, delightful boy? No! No! I sobbed it over and over as I continued to hug my imaginary Joel. I rocked back and forth on the bed, heaving with the explosive, searing pain as if a volcano had gone off in my chest. Finally, my rational mind took over.

What are you going to do now? it asked. *You're going to get up and find out what happened in the last two hours, dummy.*

I threw back the blanket and scrambled down the hall. Since I had slept in my clothes, I was fully dressed. Donning the isolation garments again, I entered Joel's room briskly.

Donna filled me in: Joel's urine output had increased—a good sign; Joel's vital signs had been stable. She thought the night nurse was a peach. Good. She had been singing to Joel most of the time I was gone. Great idea!

"Why don't you go take a shower while we do dressing changes?" Donna asked. Take a shower? That was the last thing on my mind. Last evening, Janet, another friend who had come to help, had asked me the same question, "Why don't you take a shower?"

Why in the world was everybody trying to get me into the

The Race for Survival   33

shower? One look in the mirror told all. Scratches covered my face. Soot covered everything else—soot from touching my son's charred body, soot gathered from carrying his infant seat to the waiting ambulance. I smelled like a bonfire. I looked like I had been beaten up. To the shower. . . .

As I washed my hair, I was astonished to see dried blood running down the drain. Blood? Then I recalled Mike's injury. My hair was still matted with my husband's blood!

While in the shower, I thought about our friends Jerry and Janet Krellwitz who had arrived in the middle of the night before I went to bed. I was still amazed that they had come so quickly, without reservation, to be with me. Soon after they arrived, Janet had asked me about clothes and make-up. It always irritated me that she could look so put-together no matter what she was doing. Now she was concerned about my appearance. I found this preposterous. So what if I didn't have any clothes? And make-up? What a joke! I could have cared less what I looked like.

My son could be dying, I wanted to scream at her, *and you think I should worry about how I look?* Then, though I had ignored her suggestion to take a shower, she had given me all her make-up, her electric rollers, her hair dryer, anything which I could use, from her own suitcase. She then announced that she and Jerry were taking me out to eat. What? Eat? *You've got to be kidding,* was my thought. "I don't feel the least like eating," I said. In fact, I felt sick. But they ordered me a huge meal of London broil. After the first couple bites the nausea subsided and I devoured half the food, surprised at my hunger.

Now that it was morning, I smiled to myself, thankful for their concern for me and their attention to the necessities for which I had no energy or concentration.

Sunday morning, September 16, 1979, thousands of people, representing hundreds of churches, bowed their heads in prayer for the life of Joel Sonnenberg. Some shook their fists at God and asked "Why?" Others felt the pain of that question, yet were able to trust in the Creator, the Shaper of their days, and ask for mercy— and miracles—in Joel's behalf.

On Sunday morning in Boston, Jerry and Janet Krellwitz took their trusty credit card in a desperate search for an open department store. They soon found one and began to buy things they thought Jan might need, cramming a large cardboard box with as much as it would hold—dresses, shoes, underwear, cosmetics, a huge purse, an address book, a pad of paper, a pen—anything they thought might help her. After delivering this to Jan in a whirl-wind, they went on to their next stop—New Hampshire—to check on Mike and Jami.

In Nanuet, New York, Rita Peterson sat in church waiting with the rest of the congregation for news of the Sonnenbergs. Nearly 450 people were gathered there, but the sanctuary was unusually silent.

Rita had been preparing dinner Saturday evening when the phone call came telling her that the Sonnenbergs had been in an accident and Joel was badly burned. After she hung up the receiver, Rita had prayed, thanking God for her own two young sons and for the Sonnenberg family. Remembering the strong, muscular little boy everyone called "The Hulk" of the church nursery, the little boy who had so much spunk and zest for living, she pleaded desperately, "Lord, I know You have a plan, but please, please, let Joel live! He's just a baby. How can a baby go through all that pain? How can he be so alone and so near death?"

Rita and her husband, Roy, spent the evening calling friends and family to ask for prayer for Joel. Later, they lay awake far into the night, talking, wondering about what had happened and how they would have responded if *they* had to face this tragedy themselves.

Now the pastor spoke, bringing her back to the present. "Joel Sonnenberg has made it through the night, but he has third degree burns over 85 percent of his body. The doctors have given him a 10 percent chance of survival at most."

The congregation bowed their heads as the pastor prayed, "Lord, we don't have any answers, just questions—of 'why?' But amidst all these 'whys' we remember that You are God. You have created us. You are in control of us. We lift up to You this morning

The Race for Survival   35

the Sonnenberg family in their great need. And little Joel—we can't imagine what he is going through. We know that You do, though, and that he is held in Your almighty hand. We pray for Mike, Jan, and Jami, today, for their comfort and strength. Lord, Joel's injury is so severe that we really don't know how to pray with any wisdom. We don't know which would be better—if he were to live or if he should go home to be with You. We ask only that Your will be done in this precious child's life. Amen."

As Rita heard the sobs, gasps, and sniffling of tears across the congregation, she felt again the bond called "Christian." There seemed to be a presence in that sanctuary; in the stillness she felt the awesome power of God—loving, kind, and mighty.

Someone announced that a young couple, Barb and Brian Taylor, would be driving up to Boston after the church service to take money, clothes, and other items to the Sonnenbergs. As soon as the last chords of the closing hymn were finished, the Taylors were mobbed by people handing them money and notes with words of prayer and comfort, offers of help, and just Scripture verses scribbled down hurriedly, but comfortingly meant, on scraps of paper.

The support and love of these people—Christian friends of the Sonnenbergs—seemed immense and wonderful to Rita, like a huge family. And it seemed as though the pastor had hand-picked the hymns, the Scripture readings, directed the very flow of the service to revolve around tragedy and the special need of the Sonnenbergs. Yet she knew that the printed bulletins were made up weeks in advance. Of course, she thought, God planned it. He knew. His love was being poured out for the Sonnenbergs. His Hand was guiding them through this tragedy. And His church, with its love and support and prayer would be with them in the days ahead.

"Listen, you're not his nurse—you're his mother! Why don't you start acting like one?" The outburst slapped me in the face. It came from the Sunday afternoon nurse caring for Joel. She was extremely competent in her job, and I respected her, yet I felt like yelling, *What do you know about it? Has this happened to your child? You really don't understand.* But I was also crushed. This must be my way of coping, I reasoned, but how was I acting? Was I really being that distant? It might help me to withdraw like this and be clinical, but what about Joel? Joel did need me as his mother, didn't he? Thinking as a nurse kept me in a fighting state of mind for my son; but as a mother I wasn't sure whether I wanted Joel to live or die.

One thing was certain to me: Joel would be able to sense whether I wanted him to live or die. It seemed imperative that I make up my mind—what did I want for Joel? The nurse's outburst started me thinking about my behavior as a mother toward my own badly injured child. It seemed so important for me to try and straighten these issues out, but the more I thought the more confused I became.

The phone started ringing at the nurses' desk. It seemed there were hundreds of calls for me. How exasperating it must have been for the desk clerk, yet she was always gracious. People called to say, "Our whole church prayed for Joel and you guys this morning." One friend told me that if I needed her there, she was willing to take a week off work to be with me. Relatives called from Michigan; friends called from New York. If someone had told me earlier that all these people would reach out to me in my hour of need, I don't think I would have believed it. (As a little girl, I was even shy of having birthday parties because I was afraid no one would show up!)

Then I recalled that it was Sunday. Sunday. Worship. Congregations. People. Today was the day that many, many people in New York and across the United States were praying for Joel. I tried to imagine all those prayers rising, like the thick incense I had smelled in a Catholic church, up to heaven to move the hands of God. The power of it was overwhelming—mighty.

Sunday afternoon, Barb and Brian Taylor, a young couple from our home church in New York, arrived with money, messages, clothes, and gifts. But most importantly, they brought with them the picture I had asked for—an 8 × 11 portrait of Jami and Joel sitting close together. Happy. Beautiful. Healthy. There are no words to describe my feelings as I held it and looked. This was

Joel—not that charred body lying there in the bed. This was my Joel—dressed in his summer suit, the sparkle in his eyes—my son. My beautiful son! The picture seemed to be all I really had left of him.

I quickly pasted this portrait above the head of Joel's bed. It seemed important for me to put it there for all to see—the staff, the nurses, the doctors. They had to know who they were working on—not just a charred corpse, but this wonderful, delightful child in the picture. That's who they were really working on—this wonderful child, unscarred, untouched by destruction—my boy! I sobbed and sobbed, looking at the picture. Could they see his personality? The glint of mischief in his eyes? Look at that blond hair. It was so soft. I remembered running my fingers through it. His cheeks were so pudgy you wanted to pinch them. I had kissed them over and over. He had such wonderfully thick arms. I wanted to feel those arms and the soft, plump fingers. I wanted those fingers to wrap around my hand in trust once again.

The contrast between the reality of Joel burned and the picture was overwhelming. Every time someone came into the room I motioned to the picture.

"Did you see the picture?" I would ask. "Look—that was my son! Wasn't he beautiful?" I saw many tears behind the masks of the nurses and doctors. One handsome young resident, highly intelligent, came into the room to do some procedure. When I pointed out the picture, he became very emotional and had difficulty completing the work because his hands were shaking and his eyes were blurred with tears. After finally finishing, he left the room. I never saw him again.

Joel lay there, seemingly lifeless. The machines made their noises. The nurses changed shifts. His vital signs showed little change. Joel's condition remained the same all day Sunday—stable.

In New Hampshire, Mike Sonnenberg was in great pain. His head had swollen to the size of a basketball; his severely burned hand had swollen to gigantic proportions. He could barely talk, but the phone calls which swamped him as he lay in his hospital room distracted him from his discomfort. Between calls, he kept dictating to his sister, Kathy, lists of things to do—insurance forms to be filled out, lawyers to be contacted, and possible funeral arrangements for Joel.

Doug Rupp, Kathy's husband, was hospitalized for a total of five days with painful second degree flash burns on his face and arms. During those days Kathy bore the extreme burden of trying to care for everyone: Mike her brother, whose son was probably dying, Doug her husband, and Jami her niece. She had an entire notebook filled with lists of arrangements to be made and things to do directly related to the accident.

Kathy had contacted Doug's family immediately after the accident, and word soon spread among Doug's family and friends regarding the accident the Rupps had been involved in and of the tragic situation. Doug and Kathy's church in Archbold, Ohio, joined the prayer network for Joel Sonnenberg.

In Michigan, Jan's mother had lain awake all Saturday night. "Why—why—why have You allowed this to happen to my family?" she agonized. "God, how can You do this to us? To my oldest child and my only grandson?" She took out her well-worn Bible and her favorite devotional book; she had to find something to take to Janet. She wished that her own mother, who had died five years before, was there. In lieu of that, she turned for comfort to one of her mother's favorite passages in Isaiah:

But they that wait upon the Lord shall renew their strength;
They shall mount up with wings as eagles;
They shall run, and not be weary;
They shall walk, and not faint.

It was a promise of power and renewal. Then she turned to Lamentations and read, "It is of the Lord's mercies that we are not consumed, because his compassions fail not. They are new every morning; great is thy faithfulness."

As she thought about it, Jan's mother knew that God had not caused this calamity, for it was evil and destructive. And God is good, loving, caring, and creating. Her God was so powerful, she believed, He could certainly turn evil into good. She had His promise on that. No matter what happened to Joel, God could turn it into a great thing.

Secure in that faith, she flew to Boston.

Mom arrived Sunday evening.

"Honey," she said, "Joel has been so terribly consumed by fire that it would be easy for us to just focus on the destruction. We have got to lift our minds—our thoughts—to higher things because this is just so awful we can't comprehend it. But one thing we know—Joel was miraculously saved from *complete* destruction when that young man lifted him out of the car. Joel must have been just seconds away from death. Yet he was saved. He was not totally consumed. The Lord's mercy saved him; the Lord's mercy is keeping him alive. Because the Lord has compassion, Joel is still alive.

"Now, another thing we know: Joel is still an eternal being, an ever-living soul. Joel will always be. He can't ever be totally destroyed—whether he lives or dies in the body. It will be a great mercy if Joel is taken home to be with the Lord. What greater mercy could there be than for him to be whole, free from pain and suffering, and in heaven? And yet it will a great mercy if he is spared death to live through this tragedy. Either way, we have a great mercy—whether he lives or whether he dies."

Mom and I were in the room next to Joel's where I had slept the night before. The nursing staff had set up another cot so that we could be together. Here mom talked to me, late into the night, giving me words I needed to hear, thoughts I needed to wrestle with.

"Honey, we are going to bed tonight thinking about a favorite verse of your grandmother's, Lamentations 3:22 and 23: 'It is of the Lord's mercies that we are not consumed, because his compassions fail not. They are new every morning: great is thy faithfulness.' The Lord is full of compassion and mercy because that is what is written in the Bible—He said it. That verse is ours tonight. And we are going to wake up tomorrow morning expecting a new mercy—and each morning after. Isn't that what it says? Now, maybe the mercy will be that Joel dies and goes to heaven. Maybe it will be that he is spared. But our mornings are going to give us direction for our days. Just you wait, honey. God can turn this around for good. There is nothing too difficult for God. We have a miracle-working God. That God within us is the greatest power of all. Let's direct this power for Joel."

As I lay on the hard cot in the dark hospital room, I repeated the verse mom had pressed on me: "The Lord's mercies . . . are new every morning; great is thy faithfulness."

What *would* be the greater mercy? If Joel lived, or if Joel died? It certainly was up to God, but what did I, Joel's mother, want for Joel? What did I *really* want?

If Joel lived, what would he be like? Blind? Probably. How could I cope with a blind child? Or Joel in a wheelchair, or Joel without fingers, hands, or even arms? What about brain injury? I shuddered, trying to imagine Joel as a semi-vegetable, lying in bed, unable to speak, act, even think, day in and day out for many, many years. I could not imagine a Joel devoid of spunk, sparkle, and personality. *No—no—* that was the ultimate pain. I couldn't imagine life without Joel and his spunk, his zest for living, his mischieviousness, his laughter. His arms, legs, face, his body, all could or might go—but not his mind. That I couldn't bear.

I thought about what mom had said: *Joel will always be . . . he is an eternal being . . . an ever-living soul.* This fact would not change no matter what happened to Joel physically. So even if he died, the essence, the soul, of Joel was safe.

But if he lived? A child totally changed in appearance—at the moment I couldn't even imagine what Joel looked like now after being so burned. Did I want my son to have to live like that—in whatever form eventually emerged from the devastation?

Who is Joel? I asked myself. *In addition to his soul, who is Joel really?* Was he the beautiful, plump, sturdy, blond baby boy of the picture hanging over his hospital bed? No, as precious as his face and form were to me, that was not really Joel. The real Joel was the bundle of strength, bounce, and joy who reached out so eagerly for life, who handled adversity with such twenty-two-month-old resilience. Yes, those characterstics were the living Joel; that personality was what could make him such a vital member of society. My son Joel had much to give this world.

Yes, I decided, *I want my son to live if this part of him is not touched.* My will was set.

"Yes, Lord, I want Joel spared, despite what he may look like or what handicaps he may have. If his mind is not touched, if who Joel really is, is not destroyed, please let him live."

I slept soundly that night.

The second morning I awoke in anxious anticipation. What was today's new mercy going to be? The next thought, *Will Joel die today?* hit me, and I raced down the hall to Joel's room.

The doctors were there doing morning rounds. As I waited, listening to their discussion of Joel's condition, I noticed another man gowning up to enter Joel's room. It was the ophthalmologist. He was going into Joel's room, he explained, to have a look at Joel's eyes. Joel's eyes! As the door to Joel's room shut with a thud behind him, I was frightened. What would he find? Certainly Joel's eyes had to be burned, too. My heart pounded as I wondered if his diagnosis would be, "Sorry, Mrs. Sonnenberg, your son's eyes are so badly burned that he will never see again"?

How could he even examine Joel's eyes? They were swollen shut, could he even make an accurate assessment of the damage? After the examination I was shocked to hear the physician sigh, "Well, it looks like just minor burns to the corneas, the one eye more extensive than the other."

"You mean he has his eyes?" I shouted. I couldn't believe it! I had expected the worst, and this physician seemed to be giving me wonderfully positive news. I was ecstatic. I grabbed his arm and squeezed it. I wanted to hug the man. I was so thrilled for Joel! Mike would be so excited, too. And so surprised. Hold it! Mike! Today was Mike's birthday! What a fantastic present—Joel's eyes were intact. Joel would be able to see!

The nurses began doing Joel's dressings, so mom and I went to the cafeteria for some breakfast. Afterward we noticed a courtyard outside the dining hall—a beautifully landscaped, sunny courtyard. Refreshing greenery amid concrete walls. A fountain in the middle of the courtyard shed brilliant beads of light and soothing sounds of spraying water. Mom and I sat down on a bench nearby, and as I watched the sparkling water I remembered a card I had sent to my dying grandmother years before. On it I had scribbled the Bible verse, "He that believeth on me, as the scripture hath said, out of his belly shall flow rivers of living water." I knew Jesus possessed the only living force amid our situation—amid any situation. I knew He was the giver of eternal life—as well as life here on earth.

"Honey," mom interrupted my thoughts, "I want to share with you what I believe God gave to me for you. I read these verses in my devotional book and it spoke to me especially for you.

> As one whom his mother comforteth, so will I comfort you. They brought young children to him that he should touch them
> And he took them up in his arms, put his hands upon them, and blessed them.
> I will not leave you comfortless. I will come to you. Can a woman forget her sucking child, that she should not have compassion on the son of her womb? Yea, they may forget, yet will I not forget thee.
> The Lamb which is in the midst of the throne shall feed them, and shall lead them unto living fountains of waters; and God shall wipe away all tears from their eyes."

"Honey, I have a feeling you are holding onto Joel. The only way you can truly have Joel is to give him up. Give him up to the Lord. Release him. He is a product of your and Mike's love, but God gave him to you. He is God's. Give him back—emotionally, physically. Holding on is only going to drain you and incapacitate you. It is a difficult thing to do, but it is the only way."

As I listened to mom, I looked at the nurses and doctors in white scattered around the courtyard, taking their coffee breaks. Here I was, sitting in the midst of a huge medical center complex with numerous hospitals stretching for blocks and blocks—all a part of the Harvard Medical Complex. The vast amount of knowledge represented within the radius of this complex overwhelmed me.

I can certainly trust these nurses and doctors to some degree with my son, I thought, though the extent of Joel's injuries would be taxing to the best of them. But could I trust God? Would He give Joel back to me if I gave Joel to Him? I certainly didn't know that. I was scared of what would happen if I just said, "Lord, here is my son, Joel. He's Yours. Do with him what You want—You know what is best. I'll be able to live with it either way."

Later, back up on the floor, I had a conversation with a physician that redirected my thoughts about Joel.

When I was told the plastic surgeon was on the hall, I informed the nursing staff that I wanted to speak with him. He complied with my request, and the two of us sat down on a bench in the hallway. I was immediately impressed with the intensity of this red-haired, middle-aged man who spoke tersely, rapidly, and with urgency. He seemed honest and unafraid to speak exactly what was on his mind, for I had asked him a loaded queston, "What can be done for Joel from your point of view?"

"It is imperative for Joel to be transferred to the Shriners Burn Institute across town. They are doing pioneering work in saving patients with burns the magnitude of your child's." He then explained simply, "The most important thing for Joel now is to be covered with skin. Time is of the essence. This has to be done as fast and as expertly as possible to save your son's life.

"What they will do is shave off the skin that has not been burned. Your son has good skin left on his lower back, abdomen, and buttocks. These will be his donor sites: areas which will donate the good skin to cover the rest of Joel's burned body. These skin grafts, termed 'autografts,' will be sutured in place and will grow onto his body, healing in about ten days.

"In massive burns, such as Joel's, a large area of the body must be covered with skin taken from a much smaller area. This necessitates taking many grafts from the same spot. This is called 'cropping' because the skin is harvested. The skin grows back on the donor sites and more very thin layers can then be taken off."

Cropping. Harvesting. Planting. Growing. This was farm terminology, and I understood it. But thinking of growing my son's skin as a bumper crop made me sick to my stomach. However, there was more.

The plastic surgeon explained that the skin Joel would be donating was very precious, since he really had so little of it left on his body. Therefore, the skin would be stretched to its maximum surface area by pricking tiny holes in it; this was called "meshing," as in a screen or nylon stockings.

But, the doctor stressed, the most important things now were time and fighting the germs. As soon as Joel got to Shriners Burn Institute, they would surgically remove as much of the burned tissue as was possible and cover the areas with his own skin. They must get the dead, germ-infested, burned tissue off Joel's body as quickly as possible to avoid infection. This was "primary excision."

"The treatment must begin soon," the surgeon explained, "since there is a ten-to-fourteen-day lag during which the donor sites must heal before being cropped again. Many germs can grow in two weeks, so at the Shriners Burn Institute they have pioneered the use of a skin bank; they use the skin from other individuals, termed 'allografts,' to provide temporary coverage for the burn patient. They can also take skin from either you or your husband for Joel— this skin would stay on longer than skin taken from other individuals. This is the only place in the world, that I know of, where they are using parental skin effectively to provide temporary coverage. All the allografts will eventually come off Joel because they are not his own skin—they are not grafts taken from his own body—but they'll buy time for him. These techniques reduce the percentage of body surface still open to the air and thus reduce the risk of infection."

I could have hugged this man for his information. My adrenaline was pumping again. Joel might have an even better chance at the Shriners Burn Institute!

"What do you think Joel's chances are of living if he is transferred to the Institute?"

"Well, as soon as he is covered with skin, a combination of his own and the skin bank—70 percent."

"Seventy percent! Seventy percent!" I was ecstatic.

"Now, this is something to aim for!" I exclaimed. It was such hopeful news—that Joel had a good chance of surviving if he was transferred to the Shriners Burn Institute.

"He just has to get over there!" I said. "When can he go?" I was ready. I'd leave right now!

"There may be a bed opening up tomorrow or Wednesday."

As I walked down the hall after talking with the plastic surgeon, I was approached by a short, stocky, young man.

"Hello, Mrs. Sonnenberg, my name is Mike Velardo. I am a minister." He shook my hand "My home pastor from New Hampshire called me yesterday about you. My home church is in the same town where your husband is hospitalized, and your minister in New York called him regarding your needs at this time." As we chatted, I liked what I saw and heard in this young minister. He seemed sincere, caring, with a positive, joyful attitude.

Pastor Mike suggested that he take me up to New Hampshire to visit my own Mike when I told him that today was my husband's thirty-third birthday. I never would have thought of doing this, but gladly accepted the offer. Mom said, go; she would stay with Joel.

Settling back in the comfortable front seat of Pastor Mike's car, I had second thoughts about leaving Joel. His condition was still so critical. I felt torn. I knew Mike needed me. Jami needed me. But Joel needed me, too. As we drove away from Boston, away from my son, I was already anxious to return.

It was a warm September afternoon; the sun was shining brightly; the car stereo played relaxing music in the background. Mike chatted about his work, a new child outreach in the city of Boston. He flipped on the air conditioner. My lower back got stiffer and stiffer, then started to throb with pain. We talked about my teeth—my front teeth had been chipped. Now my mouth felt funny. But at that moment I could have cared less whether I had any teeth left or not. As we neared the exit where our accident had occurred, I became more and more anxious.

Why can't we just start over again? I thought to myself. Why couldn't we all just pile into our car again, drive down this highway, and start over? Why did our little vacation have to end so suddenly, so violently, before it even started? Why did those seconds of fire have to change our lives so drastically, totally?

Mike took the exit just before the one where our accident had taken place. I was relieved. I didn't want to see the skid marks, the scorch marks, go over the same asphalt, stop at the fateful tollbooth.

Couldn't we just erase it all? Couldn't it all have been a nightmare?

The pain in my back was intense now. I bent over to try to relieve the excruciating pressue, but got no relief.

How must Joel feel? And Mike? This pain is nothing compared with theirs. And how could I even think about dental care for my teeth, I asked myself in disgust. What an insignificant thing—my teeth! My son was back in Boston, possibly dying; my daughter was being cared for by strangers; and my husband was in agony in a distant hospital room! These concerns of mine were nothing.

I noticed with surprise that Mike had pulled up in front of a dentist's office. "I'm going to see if this dentist can take care of you right now," he said, and dashed inside.

As I sat in the car, hot, heavy tears of remorse and guilt overwhelmed me for the pain of my family. *Can I go on?* I wondered. *I'm falling apart. And I don't even care.*

When Mike returned and helped me out of the car, I was still crying. While the dentist examined my teeth, I was crying.

When we got to the hospital, Pastor Mike insisted I go to the emergency room about my back. He was taking charge. I needed someone to do that for me; I just did what he said. He then escorted me upstairs to see my husband.

"Happy birthday to you . . . happy birthday to you . . . happy birthday, dear Mike . . . happy birthday to you." We had a party, complete with a beautiful cake made and decorated by Nancy MacKenzie with Jami's assistance. There were even presents and cards, beautiful shirts and sweaters from friends and from Doug and Kathy. Everyone was trying to make it a happy occasion in a very sad time.

I had not been prepared for Mike's appearance. His face was still very swollen. He had Mercurochrome all over his face, his neck, his head. Part of his hair had been shaved off. I honestly wouldn't have recognized him if I had passed him in the hallway.

There seemed to be people everywhere. Visitors. Hospital staff. Mike's mother was there helping him. Mike was in a brand-new room, also in isolation I noticed. He had two views—one of the beautiful woods outside and the other of the nurses' station. Mike would enjoy both! It was a relief to know he was receiving the best care this hospital could provide.

But I remained detached from this scene in New Hampshire. While Mike and I talked of all that was happening there with him, it seemed strange not to be talking and thinking about Joel. It was as if my body was in New Hampshire, but my mind was back in Boston.

And there was Jami, brought to the hospital by Nancy. Mike and I were both anxious to see our "Precious" as we called her. When she walked into Mike's room, he exclaimed, "Hey, Jami, how do you like all this orange crazy-foam all over my face?" She laughed, as he meant her to, hoping to relieve some of her apprehension at seeing her daddy in this state.

Shortly before Pastor Mike and I had to leave, I took Jami aside so we could have a few minutes alone together—my bouncing little girl and I. Just ten minutes alone with my daughter before I returned to Boston. We sat on the front steps of the hospital and I put my arms around her.

"Mommy, is Joel going to die?"

"Maybe Jami," I explained, looking into her huge brown eyes. "He's very sick. He was burned. If Joel does die . . . he'll be with Jesus. . . . I'm so glad you didn't get hurt, Jami."

"But, mommy, my blanket did! I left it in the car! It got all burned up!"

"We'll get you a new one, honey."

"But it won't be my blanket! Mommy, Joel was all black. Is he still black and smoky?"

"No, honey, he isn't smoky any more. . . . I'm so glad you weren't burned, that you're here on my lap, and that Nancy is taking such good care of you."

Jami Sonnenberg had been plunged into a strange, uncertain world. In the hours following the accident, she was confused and frightened, though not understanding why. First, she had run from the car, clinging to her mother. Then, snuggled in her Aunt Kathy's arms, she had watched quietly as her mother and father bent over Joel's burned, smoky body. Then more running—to the ambulance, into the hospital. There, grown-ups, strangers, rushed, hurried. People cried. Her brother, father and mother, and Uncle Doug disappeared.

In the midst of this confusion, Jami found a friend, Nancy MacKenzie. Something terrible had happened, but she was not alone. Her friend played with her and helped her draw and color pictures for her father and Joel. Nancy read stories to Jami, and they sang familiar songs. They walked down to the hospital cafeteria for milk and cookies. Nancy MacKenzie knew what Jami needed—a friend.

When Jami told Nancy that her special blanket had been burned up in the fire, Nancy called home and asked her teenage girls to find another blanket for Jami. It was important that it have blue, pink, and white in it so it would look as much as possible like the one Jami had lost. Nancy knew it was important for the little girl whose world was falling apart to have something familiar to cling to. On Saturday night, Jami slept with her new blanket at Nancy's house.

The next morning Jami wanted to talk about the accident. Nancy was wise enough *not* to say, "Not now, Jami, please don't talk about it." Or, "Just try to forget it, honey." Instead, Nancy listened intently to what Jami had to say, knowing this was one way the healing process began.

The accident was all Jami could think about—she remembered it vividly. She talked about the awful fire everywhere and about running away from it. Then there was the screaming and mommy crying. "Joel was all black, all black," Jami kept repeating. "Joel was smoky. Will he stop smoking?"

Nancy's friends from the hospital called to ask if she needed any help caring for Jami. When Nancy told them Jami needed toys to play with, they quickly brought a dollhouse with play people. Jami squealed with delight as she sorted out the little dolls. "Here's daddy, here's mommy, here's Jami!" Then her joy turned to anguish. "Where's my Joel?" she implored. There was no play brother.

Nancy's friend went out immediately and bought a "Joel" for Jami to play with. The little doll was a comfort, a promise to Jami that her family was still complete. Jami played house with the doll family, reenacting the accident again and again as she worked through her feelings. The dolls were a healing gift, enabling Jami to express what she had seen, heard, and felt.

I returned to Boston with an important present for Joel. A very small present—but one loaded with love. It was a tape recording from Mike.

I hurried up to Joel's room where mom explained how things were going and that she had been talking with pastors and singing songs to Joel between visitors.

"Joel—I'm back, honey. Mommy's back. I've been away today, but now I'm back. I'm so glad grandma was here to sing to you."

For the first time it seemed I could talk with Joel as if he weren't injured, as if I expected him to hear me. I tried to think of Joel as not being injured—as if we were back home and he was sitting on my lap.

"I went to see daddy and Jami today, Joel. Today is daddy's birthday, and we gave him presents and had a cake. They miss you very much." I started to cry. "We want you to get out of here!" I sobbed, sniffed back tears for what seemed like the hundreth time. "Right now you are in a bed in a hospital. Do you know what that is? It's a special house where people go when they are sick. You are *very* sick. There was an accident when we were in the car. A truck hit us. You were hurt. That is why you are in bed. You are resting now so that you can get well and come home."

Was Joel listening to any of this? Could he hear me? Could he hear me above the incessant beeps of the machines? And all the alarms from the machines? What was left of Joel, lying there, still spread-eagle and bound, hands, feet, arms, legs, and head, as if waiting to die—a tube down his throat breathing for him? I knew that hearing was the last sensation to leave a person. Dying people, supposedly comatose, could still hear.

"Joel!" I exclaimed. "I have a very special present for you—from daddy. Daddy wants to talk to you, Joel. Do you want to talk with daddy?"

Joel's head nodded, ever so slightly. Hold it! Was I losing my mind? Did he really do that?

"Did you see that?" I shouted to the nurse. "He nodded his head when I asked him if he wanted to listen to his daddy!"

Was I seeing things? Could Joel really respond and hear? The nurse was looking at me as if I had really flipped. Maybe I had. But it seemed as though Joel's mind was working after all. I started the tape.

"Joel, how are you, son? I love you *so* much. You know, I've been missing you. Wish we could see each other. It'd be a lot of fun being near you. Remember how we would go out in the backyard and get our hammers out and hammer on the blocks of wood? I'd give you nails so you could hammer right into the wood. Remember how you'd take the hand drill and drill little holes in the wood? That's a lot of fun, isn't it?

"Remember, too, how we'd go down to the woodpile and you'd help me split the logs and carry the logs to the big wood-pile? We got to get you out of the hospital quick so you can come home and do all that stuff.

"Remember one of your favorite things to do was go in the sandbox and make big sand castles. You know how big that sandbox is with all the sand in it. Boy—you'd take your trucks and move them around and up and down. Sometimes you'd even take your tricycle and drive it all the way from the house to the big sandbox. That was somethin' else! Sometimes when you were really trying to show off, you'd go up the hill and come speeding down, and you'd put your feet down to brake all of a sudden just before you hit the bottom of the hill.

"You know, when we get out of this hospital we're going to go for more hikes. Remember how you used to get *way* up on my shoulders and I'd lift you way high up to the sky. In fact, you had to watch out 'cause when we walked through doorway we always had to duck down or you'd bump your head. Then we'd go walking outside and we'd hike and hike and hike. Remember how you used to rub my head and my hair so softly and gently, making daddy feel so good? Yeah, that was lots of fun, wasn't it?

"Sometimes, daddy brought the green backpack along. I'd put you, Joel, in the backpack and Jami on my shoulders and we'd go for a hike. After that, we'd go on to the campus center and get the mail. Sometimes we'd even get some special envelopes that said 'Joel Sonnenberg' or 'Jami Sonnenberg.' Then we'd go down on our hike across the street. We'd hold each other very tight and look both ways and walk very slowly, listening for cars and trucks. If none were coming, we'd run across the street.

"Then, remember by the tennis courts there were logs, really railroad ties, where we would climb higher and higher and then jump down. After that we'd walk down further and then climb up again, higher and higher, and then jump down again. My! You were somethin' else!

Then we'd go way down to the beech tree. Remember how under the beech tree there was a hole in the ground. We'd put our ears down to the ground and listen to hear the trickle of water. Do you remember how much we liked to listen to the water? That was such a neat sound! We'll have times like that again, you know.

"Then daddy would go into the biology lab. Sometimes when he wasn't thinking too much, he'd even take you into the lab. You'd come into the room and get in one drawer and then another and another. Remember your favorite thing to do? You'd take those rubber stoppers and throw 'em around the room. Dad would throw up his hands in exasperation as he started searching for all those rubber stoppers because he knew Joel had been there! Then we'd start to hike back home!

"Funny boy! You liked to be outside so much! It's pretty tough being inside, isn't it. I know it's tough, but we'll get out of here and do a lot more hiking soon.

"You know another thing we need to talk about, Joel? Remember how you and Jami used to sneak quietly upstairs at our house when daddy and mommy weren't looking and you'd go into the playroom and get all the books down and dump them all over the floor. Do you remember your big truck book that you liked so much? Your truck book was so much fun! It had big pictures of trucks with headlights and wheels. Remember that, Joel? Remember how you liked all those funny people driving those trucks? Remember how you would take daddy by the hand, have him sit down on the mattress, put a book in his hand, jump up on the bed right beside him, and then with our backs against the wall we would go through the whole book. Wasn't that lots of fun?

"Daddy seems to be all talked out for a little while. Boy, am I ever excited to talk to you again. You know that we've got lots to talk about, don't we? Just lots and lots. Pretty soon I'll be talking to you again and we can tell secrets to each other—things that nobody else will know. Okay? I love you very much. Lots of hugs and kisses. Rest easy now."*

It was night again, and I was stretched out on my now-familiar cot. The scenes Mike had described on the tape played, like home movies, in my mind. There was Joel—strong, beautiful, adept at climbing, manipulating, reaching, holding. I could see him running on the grass, climbing, laughing.

The verses my mother had read to me by the fountain that morning also replayed in my mind. "They brought young children to Him that He should touch them. And He took them up in His arms, put His hands upon them, and blessed them. . . . The Lamb which is in the midst of the throne shall feed them, and shall lead them into living fountains of waters; and God shall wipe away all tears from their eyes."

I played another scene. A brand-new one. Jesus was sitting down with beautiful children on His lap. Like the Sunday school picture I had seen as a child. A picture of children clinging to Jesus, sitting on His knee, hugging His neck. And He was looking into their eyes with much love. There was Joel among them! Jesus was holding Joel with the others. Joel was happy, and he was Joel

*All excerpted from actual tape Mike Sonnenberg made for Joel.

as I had known him before the accident, as Mike had described him on the tape, and as he looked in the picture now on the wall above his bed. I clearly saw in that moment that Joel was in the very best place there ever could be—sitting on the lap of Jesus and being held by Him.

Then Jesus stood up to go, and I reached out my arms, now holding Joel, and I gave Joel to Jesus. As I lay on the cot, I actually lifted up my arms and reached out. I sobbed and sobbed as I gave up my son.

Then a gate appeared ahead of them, and Jesus and Joel walked through it togther, side by side, smiling at each other. Joel ran along, his little body jumping up and down, prancing like a little elf. He was walking, laughing, enjoying Jesus.

Then—I could no longer see them. My son! Gone! Gone! Yet with my grief came the reassuring promise that wherever Jesus took Joel, it would be the happiest place, the best place.

Outside Joel's room, the chief resident turned to me, his great sorrowful eyes meeting mine.

"It's bad news," he stated flatly, shaking his head back and forth. "He's undergoing a rapid hemolysis which must be the result of massive infection. His red blood cells are breaking down in his bloodstream. We'll try to fight it with everything we have, but it doesn't look good."

Here we go, I shuddered. Perhaps this was it. Perhaps today was the day. Infection. Acute. Massive. Sudden. Fatal.

My first reaction was to run to the phone. I called everyone I could think of, at home, in Michigan, in New Hampshire. I wanted specific prayer started for this infection.

What else could I do? I waited outside Joel's door, pacing back and forth, back and forth. Joel's room was full of people. There was a bustle of activity as a spinal tap was performed to determine whether he had an infection such as meningitis.

One of the residents came out of the room smiling. "The spinal fluid looks clear—good sign!" He was encouraged. Perhaps the infection wasn't so massive after all.

Amid all the commotion, I started at a sudden noise assaulting my ears—an electric drill whining and hammers pounding. I traced the sound. They were remodeling the nurses' station located right around the corner from Joel's room! The carpenters were working fast and furiously.

I checked my sudden impulse to run around the corner and yell, "YOU HAVE TO DO THIS WHEN MY SON IS CRITICALLY ILL? HE MIGHT BE DYING IN THERE AND YOU WANT TO REMODEL?"

Sawdust started filtering down around me; the hallway grew cloudy with it. I was furious. How dare these men bring all this dirt, crud, into the air outside my son's room? My son, so exposed, so vulernable to germs of any kind without his skin? My child lay hovering between life and death, and they had to cause this mess and racket!

I marched over to the nurses' station and registered my complaint. The hammers kept banging. The drills kept whining.

Back in Joel's room again, I started to talk to him. Soon, I ran out of words. Silence. Except for the machines. Except for the hammers and the drill. It seemed I could hardly think, so loud was the noise on the wall adjoining Joel's room. *How dare they do this?* I repeated to myself.

Suddenly, as if one of the hammers hit me over the head, *Joel loves hammers! He loves the sound of them. He loves the sounds of construction!* Mike had worked as a carpenter during the past summer vacation. Joel had loved to watch his dad hammer the boards and saw the wood when I would take the kids over to visit Mike on the job.

"Joel! Joel!" I exclaimed excitedly, hardly able to contain my enthusiasm. "Do you hear the hammers, Joel?" He nodded his head up and down very definitely—YES!

"I saw that!" the nurse exclaimed.

I couldn't believe this was happening. It seemed that God had sent the hammers for Joel. On the day he was so sick—God sent hammers! It was as if they were pounding, "Wake up, Joel!" "Wake up, Jan! Your son is alive and progressing."

Soon, the plastic surgeon walked in, the physician who had given me such encouragement the day before. I explained what the chief resident had said that morning as well as the procedures which had been performed. "They think Joel is massively infected."

"What?" he snorted. "Humbug . . . humbug," he repeated. "These children don't get massively infected until at least two weeks after the burn. Nonsense!" He bit off the words, clearly disgusted and furious, then marched out of room. I felt sorry for whoever was going to get a piece of his mind.

But I was elated! They had made a mistake! The blatant honesty of the plastic surgeon's declaration was exhilarating. Joel probably was not infected. The residents had jumped to conclusions. Rather than anger, I felt relief and excitement. This wasn't the beginning of the end!

Let the hammers pound on, Joel. We're still racing together. We're still with you son.

However, the infection incident brought up a new issue which I wanted to discuss with the nurses. If Joel's condition did deteriorate and death was near, I wanted Joel to die peacefully. I did not want some resident pounding on his chest and a team of nurses sticking him with needles.

"Do you know if there is a no-code on Joel?" I inquired of the nurse caring for Joel that afternoon. "I really would like for him to be a no-code." A "no-code" written on his chart would insure that Joel's death would be more peaceful. If God was going to save Joel, I was certain it would be without last-ditch, human resuscitative effort.

The nurse responded, "I think we would certainly respect your wishes in this case, Mrs. Sonnenberg. I think all the staff here would certainly agree to stand by your wishes."

I was relieved. Now everything seemed totally in God's hands.

I decided to make some tapes of my own for Joel. Since I was around all the time and could talk with him frequently, I thought that the best sounds Joel could hear on tape from me were songs I had sung to him before he was burned. So I recorded myself singing lullabies, hymns, and songs I had sung to Joel when I rocked him to sleep. One of the songs Joel was to hear on this tape would later hold even greater significance:

> I am a promise.
> I am a possibility.
> I am a promise
> With a capital "P."
> I'm a promise to be
> Anything God wants me to be.
> I am a promise.
> I am a possibility.
> I am a promise
> With a capital "P."

I'm a great big bundle of
Potentiality.

I can go anywhere He wants me to go,
I can be anything that He wants me to be.
I can climb a high mountain,
I can cross the wide sea.
I'm a great big promise you see.

I'm a promise to be
Anything God wants me to be.

As I sang these words into the tape recorder, they struck me.
Joel was a promise! He still had potential—lots of it. He could
lick this injury! He could win this race!

But rather than helping Joel rest to fight his burns, the tapes had
the opposite effect. As I started playing them his legs started
moving. Slowly, he lifted them. Up and down. Then vigorously,
crashing them on the bed with increased momentum and strength.
Kicking as though he was angry. Trying to communicate.

The nurse ran out. The resident ran in. After they determined
that nothing wrong physically was causing this hyperactivity, they
prescribed a tranquilizer, and Joel finally calmed down.

I tried to explain to him how important it was for him to lie
still. But he was a twenty-two month-old child, lying still, unable
to bend his arms and legs, unable to open his eyes, unable to feel
much of anything but pain beneath the bandages engulfing him;
the tube down his throat provided a better airway and breathing,
but it also prevented him from crying or screaming. Thrashing his
legs was the only form of sensation and communication left to
him.

Then, robust, efficient Rosie, one of Joel's nurses, came to me
saying, "I'm taking myself off your son's case, Mrs. Sonnenberg.
I realized last evening, while taking care of Joel, that I hadn't
gotten over the death of a little girl, also burned, I took care of
several months ago. I think these feelings are jeopardizing my
professional work with your son. And your son needs the very
best of care. So, I don't think I can care for your son any longer."

I appreciated her honesty, but I was sick. Rosie was a good nurse. Who was going to replace her? Who would do as good a job? I was disappointed, and wondered if I had done something to alienate her from Joel and myself.

The night nurse also had difficulty that evening. I was playing the tape for Joel from Mike when suddenly she sat down against the wall. She became ill, and the supervisor had to come in and take over. I felt responsible. What was I doing to these nurses? Should I stop playing the tapes to Joel? Were they affecting the staff so that they couldn't care for my son any more. I was disturbed. *Whose needs are greatest? I wondered. Joel's or the nursing staff's?* Joel certainly needed competent nurses caring for him. But he also needed demonstrations of his parents' love and care. Nurses could be replaced, to a degree, but his parents could not.

I continued playing the tapes.

Wednesday

Good news came from the plastic surgeon Wednesday morning. He marched into Joel's room and announced, "Joel will be transferred to the Shriners Burn Institute tomorrow. A bed has opened up."

Finally. I was thrilled! Joel would be in a hospital with even greater burn expertise than this one; his chances of living had to be even better there.

It began to bother me, however, that I had no idea of the implications of this injury to our total family. How long would Joel be alive? How long would he be in the hospital if he lived? Would our medical insurance cover all these expenses? How would we ever be able to afford all the costs over a lifetime if Joel did survive?

Since the day of the accident the question of money had surfaced in my mind, but I had continually pushed it down. So what if Mike and I went bankrupt? We didn't have that much money to begin with—professors are not known for being highly paid. I didn't care if Joel's expenses took everything and we were in debt forever. I just wanted him to live—that's all that mattered. Yet, in reality, it did matter what change in lifestyle this race for life represented for the rest of us.

Mom and I met with the social worker on Wednesday morning, and I brought up my concerns about expenses and the long-term financial instability that might be facing us. "How do families cope with this constant drain on their resources over a long period of time?" I asked. "You shouldn't have too much problem with that since Shriners Burn Institute is free," she said.

"WHAT?" I practically bolted out of my chair. "DID YOU SAY *FREE*—no cost?" Free?

"I'm almost positive—I'll check further into it today for you, but I'm sure it's free."

"How can it be free?" I asked.

"It is funded by the work of the Shriners of North America. You've seen the Shriners in parades haven't you?"

"Yes, but I don't know anything about them."

"They are thousands of men across the United States in a brotherhood, like a fraternity or a large club, broken down into local units. Through their charitable work, such as the Shrine Circus, these men raise monies to help children. The Burn Institute in Boston is just one of many hospitals they totally support in their work with burned and crippled children."

Mom and I vowed that as soon as we were over at the Institute we would run up and kiss the first Shriner we saw! Such wonderful men! Free care!

The social worker continued, "There is no place for parents to stay overnight with their children at the Institute, so you won't be able to stay with Joel as you have been doing here. You'll have to find residence elsewhere." She handed me the name and telephone number of a convent near the Institute where parents often stayed when they needed housing over a length of time.

Separation from Joel seemed inevitable. How could I stand it? How could I bear not being near my injured son all the time? Not there in case something happened? Not there in case he needed me?

I was frightened at the prospect of being separated from Joel.

Thursday

"Joel, this morning we are taking you to a new hospital. A new house where there will be other children who are sick, too. It is a better house for you to be in, and you are going to get well faster there. Mommy will be there, too. The doctor is going with you; so are two nurses and a lady to help you breathe better. Everyone wants you to get better. I'll see you again after you get to the new house."

Of course, with this entire team of medical personnel accompanying Joel to the Shriners Burn Institute, there was no way I was going to fit into the ambulance! As it was they were packed in like sardines. I got the feeling everyone was excited for Joel. Part of it was probably relief that they didn't have to care for him any more, but I did sense an optimism as I accompanied the team, with Joel being wheeled on a stretcher, into the elevator, down the hall, and out the front doors to the waiting ambulance.

As they all climbed into the ambulance with my son, I felt the beat of excitement, exhilaration, challenge. Again we were journeying out into the maze of streets known as Boston, just as we had done five nights previously, but this time our destination was definite and our course of travel clear.

As Pastor Mike drove mom and me over to this new hospital in his car, I reflected on what the physician had said earlier that morning.

"Mrs. Sonnenberg, I just talked with a physician at Shriners. The transfer is taking place this morning, as you know. They are sending over an ambulance to pick up your son. When I told him you were a nurse, he said that you would be allowed to ride in the ambulance with your son."

"Allowed?" I said. *Allowed?* I repeated to myself. *Allowed to be with my son?* This surely was my right, not a privilege! I simmered indignantly at this message.

Little did I know that this short message from the resident physician regarding the ambulance ride would be the beginning of a deep struggle, not easily resolved.

Inside the lobby of the Shriners Burn Institute, mom and I walked around, examining our new surroundings, the large collage of life-size pictures hanging on a stretch of wall grieved me. They were beautiful children, their bodies a wonder of perfection. One blond-haired child was naked, lying on the sand at the beach. One young boy was swinging a bat. Beautiful children. Perfect. Joel had been that way once. Could he ever look like that again. My son, upstairs, burned to a crisp—would he ever look like that again?

No doubt they were working on him right now. What were they doing? The resident had mentioned that this hospital had its own techniques, its own way of doing things. Everything had to be done exactly according to procedures they prescribed. What was going on upstairs? What were they doing to Joel? A glass case in the corner of the room caught my eye. Inside this case was a large, gold book. The inscription read:

In this Book of Gold are recorded the names of those who have been mercifully mindful of little children who needed help.
For them we pray God's blessings.
Dedicated to those who have aided in our work
Shriners Burn Institute
Boston Unit

I was in awe of this book. I was in awe of this hospital. I wanted to open up the case and write down the names and addresses of these people and send them a letter of great appreciation. But, of course, that was impossible. Besides, since the names written therein were persons who had made gifts to the hospital by leaving money in their wills, it might be pretty tough to get in touch with them!

The first nurse I was introduced to at the Institute was the head nurse, who came down to greet and orient me. I felt depressed after meeting her. She seemed concerned to inform me of all the rules. Rules for this, rules for that. Under the pressure of these moments, the term "visiting hours" slapped me in the face. *Visiting hours? We are living in 1979 aren't we? Visiting hours—in a children's hospital? I'm now a visitor?* From my perspective, it seemed I was being controlled and regulated.

The head nurse informed me that I could go upstairs to see Joel only when told I could by the receptionist at the front desk. The receptionist would first call the floor, and the staff there would give or deny permission. I wanted to yell, "I'm not Joel's visitor. I'm his mother. I belong with my son!" I felt as if someone had yanked my son out of my arms without my permission. Indeed, it seemed they had taken him away from me.

Despite these misgivings, I firmly believed Joel was in the best institution to save his life. I knew his survival did depend on the expertise found within the walls of this great research hospital, the Shriners Burn Institute.

Ruth Brescia lived in the northern Boston suburbs. Her parents lived in Indiana and were friends of Doug and Kathy Rupp. When Ruth learned about the accident, she immediately offered her home and care to Jan and her mother.

Thursday night, Joel's first night at Shriners, Jan and her mother stayed with Ruth for the first time.

For the next two weeks Ruth transported the two women back and forth to Boston. With the help of members from her Congregational church, she cooked their breakfast and supper, did laundry and shopping, and answered all the telephone calls. Ruth, though a nurse herself, could not comprehend the magnitude of Joel's injury or the circumstances surrounding it, but she wisely discerned that Jan needed to be freed from as many mundane tasks as possible so that her energy would be available for coping with caring for Joel and Mike.

Mike's sister Nancy now flew up from Kentucky with her four-year-old son, B.J., to care for Jami. Mike and Jan had decided that while Mike remained hospitalized and Joel's critical condition demanded all of Jan's energy and attention, the best place for Jami was in her own home in New York. For Jami, this meant a return to a familiar world—her own bed, her own toys, her own yard, her own playmates—and to the additional security of being cared for by her aunt.

When the team that had escorted Joel to Shriners' came downstairs, they flocked around me to say good-by. Our time together had been short, but the intensity of the crisis had forged a bond.

"I have a good feeling about your son. I think he's going to make it," the resident said as he left, smiling.

As I watched them walk out to the cab, I felt alone, abandoned.

I asked a staff member, "When do the physicians talk with parents here?"

"You can sometimes catch the physicians up on the floor. They usually are in the operating room, caring for patients, or in meetings. Most parents have found it best to wait down here in the lobby at around 5:00 P.M. That's when many of the doctors are leaving the building, and you can usually catch them on their way out if you have a question." I was absolutely dumbfounded at this information.

At the time, the only reply I could muster was, "Me? Chase after a physician to drag out information regarding my dying child?" Here was Joel, so terribly devastated, with such an unusually severe injury, and I had to force these doctors to talk with me? They should *want* to inform *me*! I was Joel's mother—I was important to Joel.

From my perspective, at that time it seemed the physicians were concerned with operating on Joel, planning surgeries and medical interventions—all part of their vital care for Joel—but did not care about informing his family of plans, priorities, or problems. I grew angry, resentful that such intelligent people could be so wrong.

My indignation was interrupted by the receptionist calling me to go upstairs to see Joel.

On the third floor in the east wing, the intensive care side of the hospital, things were bustling—the atmosphere electrified with a sense of urgency. Here I was introduced to Joel's new residence, a plastic tent termed a "Bacteria Controlled Nursing Unit," abbreviated B.C.N.U. It was a unit pioneered there at the Institute.

The smooth, durable, plastic tent encased my son. To approach him at all, I needed to don more plastic: on my arms, up to my shoulders, went large, thin but bulky gloves, followed by a pair of surgical gloves; in addition, a plastic gown covered my clothes while a mask completed the mummy look. And with all this, I still could only see Joel through a wall of plastic, completing the distortion of sight and sound.

The staff explained to me that these plastic units were the most effective control found to reduce the risk of infection by isolating children from the germs of other patients, visitors, and staff. The air entered the top of the unit and was filtered before flowing over the patients, thus making it bacteria free; the air was then filtered again as it passed out of the system near the floor. Also, the temperature and humidity in the plastic unit were precisely controlled. These precise, sterile techniques were part of what accounted for the Institute's success with burn victims.

There were four plastic units in Joel's large, open ward. Each unit contained a severely burned child. The ward also contained four or five other beds. The bombardment of noise and activity was tremendous.

Already I missed Joel's private room back at the other medical center. I felt helpless in the midst of this scene of swirling competency. I felt completely exposed in the large, open ward where my every move could be watched and my conversation overheard; it seemed I no longer even had the privacy to cry. I wanted to be enclosed again in a small room with four walls for protection, for privacy, for some sense of identity. My anxiety grew as I thought of the impact of all this confusion and noise on Joel, my little son, trapped in his crib, immobilized and in pain. Furthermore, I didn't feel totally safe talking with the nurses or other staff members; I was afraid my feelings would become common knowledge in this small hospital with its large, exposed rooms.

"Mrs. Sonnenberg, we're going to do dressing changes now. Perhaps it'll take an hour or more. Could you go downstairs, and we'll call you when you can come up again." It was the assistant head nurse speaking, smiling. Her friendly cheerfulness was soothing.

Down in the lobby I began the first in what was to seem an unending marathon. Waiting. In another large room—the lobby. There was no place I could even wait without feeling vulnerable.

Later, back upstairs, after a few hours at Joel's bedside I asked again if I would be talking with one of the physicians soon. A nurse explained that one of the residents would probably be available and that they could arrange it for me.

Soon I was ushered into an office in the back of the ward. I was excited, hopeful, and relieved that Joel was finally at the Institute. Now I wanted to hear from this physician about the increased chances of my son's survival since he had entered this excellent world-renowned treatment center for burns. I fully expected to discuss donating skin and the 70 percent recovery rate the plastic surgeon at the other hospital had discussed with me previously.

Sitting at his desk, leaning back confidently in his chair was a handsome, blond, resident physician. His manner was crisp, his eyes cold and distant. He spoke to me without emotion in choppy sentences as I introduced myself.

"Joel's chances were deemed around 10 percent when he entered the emergency room right after our accident," I said. "What would you say they are now?"

Without hesitation he replied, "Oh, around 5 percent."

Five percent! Either this guy was crazy or I was. What was happening here? Was someone lying to protect his own interests? I wanted accurate information based on sound data. The discrepancy in these percentages was preposterous! I was going right to the top!

In no time I marched into the office of the chief of staff. He didn't seem too surprised to see me, just somewhat cautious since I had burst right in. I explained to him the two opinions I had heard. I asked for clarification—it was important for me to fully understand how much hope to maintain realistically in my son's race for life.

"I would say two out of three of our patients who are burned as extensively as your son survive at Shriners," he said.

I breathed a sigh of relief and left his office with a sincere, "Thank you."

Back on the unit I asked Joel's afternoon nurse his opinion, too. The nursing staff would probably level with me, so I told him of my conversation with the resident and with the chief of staff. As I had hoped, his answer was honest.

"I don't think I would say the percentages are as good as two out of three—I would say 50-50, maybe less." The nurse's eyes shifted and his head lowered as he continued, "One thing I have to tell you, Mrs. Sonnenberg—never think that your son has made it until he gets out of this plastic tent. I recently worked on a boy with an even more extensive burn than Joel's. We lost him—I still don't think I'm over it. So for your sake, don't ever think the race for survival is over until it really is.

Friday

On Friday morning Mike Sonnenberg stared out the window of his hospital room in New Hampshire. Today he would be transferred to Boston.

At Mike's birthday gathering, Pastor Velardo had suggested that Mike be transferred to Boston so he could be nearer Jan and Joel. This small step toward reuniting the scattered Sonnenberg family would also insure continued expert treatment of Mike's injury. It had taken four days to complete the arrangements to move Mike to the burn unit of a large Boston medical center. Friday morning had been set for the transfer. Despite his terrible pain, this week had been busy for Mike—crammed full of decisions and visitors. He had talked to so many people he felt talked out.

Last night Mike had lain awake thinking about being closer to Jan and Joel and disturbed by the pain of his own injuries. He thought he should be on the mend by now and feeling at least a little better. Instead, he felt worse every day. What about Joel? he thought. What was he feeling? Joel was burned like this all over his body. If he felt like this, what must Joel feel? Mike wondered if he would ever feel good. Would Joel? Would he ever see his son again?

Noticing again the lush woods directly outside his window and the beginning of the fall foliage, Mike wondered what new setting awaited him in Boston? He would miss the country landscape. He keenly missed being active and outdoors. When he had been admitted, his physician had said he would be out of the hospital in ten days. Perhaps he would only be confined for another week in Boston. He certainly hoped so. He wanted to be with his wife and son.

On the journey to Boston, Mike's pain was so intense he didn't think he could survive the trip. The ambulance driver showed his concern by slowing down to ten miles per hour, even on the expressway, but even at that speed the ride was agony. Each jolt of the ambulance, each bump on the road, sent waves of pain through Mike's body.

I forgot all about Mike's transfer Friday morning, for the day began with Joel's first major operation at the Shriners Burn Institute. They were beginning to cover Joel with skin. But would the operation jeopardize his life? Would he survive it?

I waited for hours downstairs in the lobby. Sometimes the room was filled with outpatients—crying children, beautiful children. It was difficult to look at them—particularly the extra beautiful ones, the ones who looked like Joel, blond-haired, healthy, robust little boys. As I watched them run and play, it seemed I was seeing Joel again. But of course I wasn't. Could he ever look like these boys again? I felt loss, but expectancy. If God could save my son's life, certainly He could make some provision for putting him back together!

The receptionist interrupted my thoughts by calling, "Mrs. Sonnenberg, you have a phone call."

Who could be calling while Joel was still in surgery?

"Jan, how are you? It's mom." It was Mike's mother.

"Hi, mom . . . where are you?"

"Here in Boston at the hospital with Mike. We've just arrived and they've taken him upstairs."

I was shocked. "Oh—" I'd forgotten all about Mike's transfer, so absorbed was I with Joel's first surgery! "How is he?"

"He had a hard time during the ambulance ride. I've never seen him so miserable. But the driver and the nurse were very kind and helped him as much as they could. It'll be awhile before he's settled."

After Mike's mother hung up, I immediately called the nurses' desk of the burn unit where Mike was to be admitted.

"Hello, this is Mrs. Sonnenberg. My husband, Mike, was to be transferred from New Hampshire today via ambulance and admitted to your burn unit. Has he arrived on the floor yet?"

"Yes, he's here, but you can't see him yet. He's being worked on in his room."

"What are they doing?"

"Getting him ready."

"Ready for what?"

"They have to examine him and do dressing changes. Look, why don't you call back later?"

I was still waiting in the lobby to hear about the outcome of Joel's surgery, expecting one of the physicians to come down and inform me about my son. I could have waited all day—no one ever came!

Finally the receptionist said I was allowed to go upstairs. After checking in on Joel, who was still sedated from the anesthesia, I again called about Mike. I called and called.

"He's not ready yet," was repeated over and over to me. What in the world could be taking so much time?

Finally, "Yes, you can come over now."

I was able to walk to the medical center where my husband was being treated.

At the hospital I had to go through the dressing-up routine again—the sterile conditions necessary for burn victims. But these gowns were heavy, cumbersome cloth garments, very hot. Opening the door of Mike's private room, I was startled by the man lying semi-upright in bed. I had talked with Mike often on the telephone in the last five days, but I had seen him only once. He was completely changed from four days ago.

His head, arms, and torso were wrapped with gauze bandages. His hand was bound to a board which extended up under his arm. His face was covered with Mercurochrome and contorted in pain. He was moaning. And he was in one of the drabbest hospital rooms I had ever seen.

"Hi, honey. How are you?"

"Awful. No—don't touch me! What took you so long to get over here?"

"They wouldn't let me in before this."

"My hand hurts so bad, I want to die. They debrided my hand. Why can't they give me more morphine? It didn't touch the pain. Please help me—lift up my leg—ooh!" he cried. "Not so fast! Go slowly—slowly," he whined.

I had never seen Mike like this before. He was always on top of every situation. I had never seen him so contorted with pain.

What was worse, I seemed helpless to do anything to make him feel better.

"The ambulance ride was the worst experience of my life. Those are the bumpiest roads I've ever seen. We must have hit every hole between New Hampshire and Boston. I thought I would die."

"Honey, at least you're here now and we're closer together. Joel had surgery today. They covered his back. They gave him a lot of blood."

"How is he doing?"

"He's still under the anesthesia."

"Oh, good, at least he's out of pain for awhile," Mike rasped.

"What did the doctors say about your burns?"

" 'We'll wait and see,' they say—which means nothing. Everything is so different here. The procedures are all different. They were even talking about operating—that I might need grafts on my hand and shoulder."

"Mike, they must know their stuff because this is one of the best places in the world for burn treatment. What can I do to help you? Oh—look at all these cards you brought with you—it's unbelievable!"

"See if you can find out if I can have more medication," Mike groaned, his face bathed in sweat.

The Race
with
Suffering

The First Weeks

After the first sprint for survival—the establishment of breathing, the stabilization of body fluids—the race against infection began in earnest. Joel was badly burned over 85 percent of his body, leaving a massive area of tissue open to infection. Thus, he needed to be covered with his own unburned skin as quickly as possible. Within the first week of Joel's hospitalization at Shriners Burn Institute, he underwent three extensive operations—each lasting three to five hours—which began the process of covering him with his own skin. The idea was to perform as many surgeries as possible as quickly as possible, since the body's tolerance of multiple surgeries decreases over time.

Covering Joel's burned body with skin was no small task; only 15 percent of his body remained unburned. This meant that grafts of Joel's skin would have to be supplemented with grafts of skin from Mike's body. Over the next few weeks we faced a fast and furious series of operations in the race to cover Joel's back, chest, legs, and arms with skin grafts. Our race centered around surgeries, anxiety over whether the grafts would "take" (that is, heal onto his body), and fear of infection—a fear made more agonizing by the fluctuations of Joel's temperature.

Joel's first operation was performed the day after he was admitted to Shriners. In this operation, his back—almost totally burned—was covered with skin taken from his abdomen. First the charred tissue or eschar was cut away; then, skin-graft, meshed and stretched, was placed on the exposed tissues. Joel lost a great deal of blood—at least four units for each large area being grafted. In such a young child this meant they replaced his total blood volume almost twice.

It was important that Joel's body "take" as much of each graft as possible. If a large amount did not heal onto his body, it meant further delay in covering Joel with skin. And the more time it took to get that precious covering on, the greater the chance of infection and death.

The next surgery, three days later, covered Joel's chest—more extensively burned than his back—with his own skin. Four days after this, Joel's legs, burned "circumferentially"—that is, all the way around, were grafted with skin donated from Mike's thighs. This temporary graft would protect Joel from germs and prepare the underlying tissue to receive a later graft of his own skin. Because this skin graft came from Mike, Joel needed to take an immunosuppressant, a medicine which lowers the body's ability to fight foreign objects—his father's skin tissue and germs. It was important that Mike's skin stay on Joel's body until the next layer of Joel's own skin could be used.

Next they began to graft skin from Mike onto Joel's arms. As the surgeries followed one another at a challenging pace, I began to feel emotionally drained. The stress of anxiety over Joel was continuous. Would he live through the next operation? Was he in danger of contracting hepatitis from all that donated blood? The evenings before each surgery were especially difficult, but the days after the operations were hardly better. Joel's temperature continued to fluctuate, especially after he received Mike's skin. He ran a fever every day; sometimes it peaked in the afternoon at 104° - 105°, only to rise again at night.

Often as Joel's temperature soared he became restless and needed to be restrained. The nurses had to tie his arms and legs to the sides of the bed to keep him from injuring himself further. Watching Joel's agony was terrible enough, but having to leave him was worse. And often just as his temperature began to rise in the evening, I had to leave because visiting hours were over. After an hour away from Joel I wouldn't be able to stand it any longer and would have to call in to ask the nurses if Joel's fever had gone down. Each time, I was afraid the fever was the beginning of the end. Would my Joel become a morbid statistic?

During those days when they were racing to get Joel's burns covered with skin, the strain on the staff of highly trained nurses and physicians was tremendous. Because, of course, my Joel was only one of many severely burned children in the Institute. The operating room was in constant use. Often the children due for reconstructive surgery, the primary task of the rehabilitative side of the hospital, had their operations postponed so that crucial surgery could be performed on children fighting for their lives. The entire hospital seemed to be constantly hovering over these dear, young, precious children, so precariously balanced between life and death. *To me* it seemed like the whole world was watching, waiting, praying, hoping, listening for word of one little boy— Joel Sonnenberg.

October

October held days filled to capacity. So many people visited: both my sisters as well as my parents, twice; friends from New York as well as students who doted on Mike as their favorite professor; Mike's sister and mother traveled back and forth from New York and Kentucky; Jami traveled back and forth from Nyack. There was a lot of mail—most of which I never answered, but was extremely grateful to receive. There were hundreds of phone calls.

And all the time I had the feeling that many, many people were watching me—my fellow professionals as well as our friends. I felt enormous pressue to "do well." When someone said, "My, but you're doing so well!" I wondered what they meant. What was "doing well"? What specific behavior were they talking about? Because I didn't cry in front of them? Because I wasn't angry all the time? Because I smiled?

All I knew was that I was doing the best I could and that I would continue to do it because I had to keep running. The stakes were so high: for Joel, but also for myself. I didn't want to live thinking, if only I had given a little more—done just one more thing—given Joel a few more hugs or read him a few more stories, maybe he would have made it. I didn't want to be left with guilt over failing to put forth the supreme effort. I wanted the "what ifs" kept to a minimum. I was clearly racing to do anything I could for Joel. It was the greatest race I would ever run. The odds were against us and the course sometimes unclear, but there seemed to be many on the sidelines cheering me on, cheering Joel on, cheering Mike on. But I needed to have someone say, "Jan, I like you just the way you are—falling apart at the seams, putting up a good front, or just struggling along. Behave any way you want—I'll cheer you on because I believe in you that much."

During these weeks in October, I fled at night to St. Margaret's Episcopal Convent, a convent on Beacon Hill—a place where time had stopped, it seemed, at the turn of the century. As I walked Beacon Hill's cobblestone streets with its brick townhouses and gaslights, I could almost see the top-hatted gentlemen, the bridled horses pulling buggies through the rainy nights.

The crisp fall leaves floating down, and the view of the Charles River were lovely sights to behold, but as I drank them in, I thought mostly of the beauty that Joel was missing or that Mike couldn't think of because he was so absorbed in his own pain and Joel's, or the fact that Jami wasn't with us and that our family was torn apart. What about next fall? What would it bring? These questions scared me.

At the convent, prayer and silence were the order of every day, and this quiet life was calming. Sometimes it seemed my circuits were overloaded like a jammed computer. I needed to be alone with my thoughts, to be relieved from the pressure of talking with people or caring for others physically or emotionally.

The convent halls were soothing. The only sounds were leather heels on solid wood, echoed chimes from the chapel, soft voices of kind nuns. At breakfast only the ring of metal spoons on earthern bowls, the gulp of strong coffee—and SILENCE. I loved it. It seemed I was truly prepared for another day.

Tucked away in the quiet of the convent one night, I sat at my desk as I usually did in the evenings. It was way past nine o'clock, when the Great Silence (no speaking until after breakfast in the morning) began. The light from the small desk lamp cast shadows around the tiny room with its lumpy cot and drab green-gray walls. Looking out my window, I saw the Back Bay section of Boston brightly lit against the night sky and the moonlit Charles River that was somehow ghostly but beautiful, awesome. I bent over my desk again trying to concentrate. I needed to fill out accident reports for the New Hampshire State Police, objectively writing down my version of the accident so that someone sitting at a desk up in New Hampshire could read through it quickly and know exactly what had taken place—from my point of view.

What had taken place? I had to take myself back to September 15. "Vehicle driven by so-and-so did such-and-such . . . ." Injuries sustained? "Mike Sonnenberg . . . burns to this and that part of the body. . . . Joel Sonnenberg . . . severe and massive third degree burns . . . condition still critical. . . ." Write it down, quickly, efficiently. But not a true picture of those moments in time when a family's life is changed forever by the impact of rolling steel. How could anyone really write the pain of it? The horror? The grief? The fire's ruin?

The report leveled me. Writing words that needed crispness, black and white detail, start and finish, was not that simple. How dare anyone throw into a file the lives and pain of my husband and son?

I snapped off the light and threw myself on the lumpy cot. The ceiling hung high and empty above me. I could see the shadowed form of the crucifix on the wall above my bed. I couldn't sleep. I thought about my days. The hustle and bustle. The brightness of hospital lights, the noise of machines, the plastic layers of protection against germs. The fast-paced work of the nurses. The racing of minds and bodies to save children's lives. Pressure. Time. Voices. Noise. Hurry, hurry. Hurry over to visit Mike. Try to keep him happy. Hurry back to visit Joel. Hurry to answer the phone. Think of something to do for Joel today to make his day better. Keep up the pace. Don't lose your cool—think about the fever spikes, the layers of skin, the layers of covering for Joel. Cover—protection— like this blanket covering my body now. Joel needed to be covered—couldn't it go faster, quicker, farther? God could do this for Joel. Like a blanket smoothed over his body. Yes, like the blanket over me now. But didn't I need covering, too? How could I go on like this? Worrying about Joel, Mike, Jami, reports, finances, visitors, correspondence. Thank-yous to write. People to smile at. I need coverage! Protection! I think I'm going insane! I'm exhausted!

"Lord, I don't think I can go on like this. I don't think I want tomorrow to come. I can't do all this myself. I'm not as independent as I thought I was. I need You. I need strength. I'm so tired I can't get off this cot. I feel like a sack of cement. I'm carrying too much weight. Will You take some of it off?

The heaviest is Joel—he weighs me down. Only You can cover him with skin—fast, sure—to save his life. I'm giving him to You again, just as I did in those first days after he was burned when

I lay on another cot and he was in another hospital. Here he is—I give his body to You. Only You know what's going on. You know everything—about his temperatures, his behavior, all that is going on with him. Here he is. He's Yours."

I lifted up my arms again, as if handing the body of my son to Jesus to carry. I was sobbing again. Would the tears never end? How could I cry so much? Yet at other times not enough?

As I handed Joel over to Jesus, I felt a presence—arms around me, holding me up so I felt light but strong. No longer a sack of cement. New strength—that wasn't mine—to face tomorrow. New energy with which to run.

Back in his small, private hospital room, Mike was running his own race, and sometimes it seemed he was running alone against his pain, depression, and frustration.

During one operation surgeons cropped about three square feet of unburned skin from his thighs to use as grafts for Mike's own severe burns and for Joel's. The pain of these donor sites—where skin is shaved off to be grafted onto burn sites—was excruciatingly painful. It was as if a hot iron had been held against his thighs, then removed, leaving an intense pain that lingered for days and for which there was little relief.

Mike, usually a disciplined, in-charge person, felt his life slipping from his control. Daily his frustration and anger mounted. He grasped at anything that might alleviate his helplessness, even simple, routine matters. When his call light wasn't answered, he flung plastic dishes from his dinner tray out into the hallway to get the attention of the nurses. This of course brought their much-needed presence—and the bedpan.

When he asked one nurse to go more slowly as she ripped off his dressings, she went even faster. This, on top of her usual sour manner and disregard of his requests, was too much. He shoved her away, slamming her against the wall of his room.

Mike's pain was a source of double agony. He was suffering physically and tormented by his dependence on others. But his pain was also a constant reminder of Joel's suffering, and his separation from him. Joel, too, was burned, and much more severely. Joel, too, was enduring the pain of donor sites. Mike could not be at his son's side in those first days of his race for survival, but he was suffering every step of the way with him.

Mike Sonnenberg was a very special person to many people— a hard man to forget. So when news of his accident and the serious injury of his son began to spread, the network of people who knew and loved Mike went to work.

Many of Mike's students at Nyack College called their parents and notified the pastors of their home churches so people could pray for Joel. Faculty and staff members of the college did the same. A week after the accident, as pastors representing congregations throughout New England were gathered for the area conference of the Christian and Missionary Alliance denomination, they bowed their hearts in prayer for Joel, then went home and asked their congregations to pray. More prayer lights were coming on all across the country as the news spread to friends and relatives of these students, faculty, staff, and pastors.

Mike had earned his undergraduate degree at Taylor University in Indiana. People there remembered Mike's disciplined life, his academic and athletic excellence, his Christian commitment. They, too, began to pray when they heard the news. And they contacted others. Soon Mike was hearing from classmates in California, Wyoming, Oregon, Texas—some he hadn't talked to since graduation ten years before. After his classmates had expressed their sorrow for Mike and his family, they often asked him about his life and told of theirs. Mike enjoyed his "shop talk" with friends who were now physicians, professors, businessmen, pastors; it was a welcome respite from the pain. One former football buddy said: "Mike, I hurt all over for you. Worse than when we rammed the line together." Friends who remembered Mike's love of laughter sent joke books. His body hurt more when he laughed, but that laughter was healing for his spirit.

Mike continued to hear from current and former students who had not forgotten his concern for them. One wrote; "I guess it's just another idiotic trait of human beings that we wait until a moment of maximum emotion before expressing our feelings. All those great times in your class constitute much of what I consider my most valuable education . . . . I have learned so much from you, so much that's really important and lasting and I want you to know that I'm very, very grateful."

In the early weeks of Joel's hospitalization it seemed important to promote a quiet and peaceful environment for him, one conducive to rest. Also, my presence as well as Mike's verbal presence through tapes must reassure Joel of our love and care for him—that mommy and daddy did love him and would be there and continue to help him in any way we could. We didn't know how much Joel understood of what had happened to him—only twenty-two months old. So we decided to treat our son, play with him, and explain things to him just as though he was still the same Joel—the same little boy who had not been burned. We didn't know if his personality was intact, but we had nothing to lose and everything to gain, and so did Joel, if we assumed he was mentally the same.

Slowly, small portions of Joel started to show themselves. First, his eyes emerged as the dead, burned tissue began to shrink and fall off. His eyes were open; they shifted to the right and the left. He was able to shake his head up and down. We could tell that he could understand our questions. With the rest of his body so hidden by bandages, I was overjoyed when I could see his eyes. Above all, it was good to know that Joel now had a sensory input of some sort besides hearing. But what could he see from inside his tent of plastic? What must my face look like to him? Did I look like his mommy?

Two days after his eyes became visible, his airway was taken out. Slowly and surely the nursing staff had been striving to wean Joel off the respirator for days, extremely important for his total rehabilitation. The longer he was dependent on the respirator, the longer his recuperation would take and the more danger there was of permanent damage to his lungs and throat.

I can't describe how I felt when I heard Joel cry for the first time since he had been hospitalized. "Here's my son!" I wanted to yell to the whole ward. "He's back! Joel's back! I thought he was dead—now he is back!" Such a small happening, but what a great encouragement to a mother desperate for signs of her son's progress.

Joel had said only three words before the accident—"daddy," "mommy," and "bobble." Now Joel's first word when the respiratory tube came out? A raspy, "Daddy, daddy, daddy," and he cried it over and over and over. I was heartbroken for him, unable to answer this small demand to have his daddy near in the midst of his pain.

Several days later we faced the full impact of Joel's freedom from the respirator. It was morning. The nurse was trying to do his dressing changes and make his bed. Though bound hand and foot in heavy stiffening splints, Joel was standing up in bed, screaming, thrashing, pulling out the tube through his nose for feedings into his stomach—he was totally out of control. He was angry. He didn't understand. He wanted to get out of there. Off the respirator, he had more freedom, and he was going to show everybody exactly what he wanted!

With this measure of freedom came a challenge. Joel could see now. He could look around the inside of the B.C.N.U. He could scream and yell if he wanted to. But he was flat on his back, with his head slightly elevated; he was bound—head, feet, and arms—with bandages and splints. He still looked like a little mummy lying there.

He wanted to move around, wanted to scream and yell. He was hurting. He was angry. He wanted to get out of the tent. As he kicked and screamed it seemed he was saying, "Mommy, get me out of here. Take me home. I don't like it here. People hurt me. I'm scared."

In the weeks ahead, the challenge and focus of running with

Joel was how to keep him calm, yet stimulate him mentally. How to play with him without provoking restlessness and anxiety. If he became too restless, he might rub his graft sites so hard that they wouldn't heal, thereby jeopardizing his life even further.

But along with my concern came excitement—for each new challenge meant a little more of Joel was being returned to me. For example, his giggle. Mom and I stopped at a bookstore one morning, looking for Joel's favorite books. Since it was important for all of Joel's toys to be brand-new to minimize germs, familiar books or toys could not be brought from home into the hospital. So we went out looking for the favorite things he had at home. We found two of his favorite books, both very colorful. One was about huge trucks. Another was a "do" book about animals; Joel had enjoyed turning up the windows or doors which covered up the animals, playing peek-a-boo with them.

We also bought three or four other books he had never seen. One of these was about boats, and it had action—lots of it. When the boats were manipulated up and down by the tabs, they did funny, crazy things. It was a three-dimensional picture book. I was eager to show Joel these wonderful new presents.

Entering the unit upon our return, I approached Joel's bed after washing my hands thoroughly at the nursing station and donning the plastic apparel. I then proceeded to the foot of Joel's bed where I, as always, read his flow-chart to check on his physical progress of the last hours.

Then I reached into the unit and leaned my whole body into the plastic wall, trying to move it out of the way as much as possible to get closer to my son. "Hi, Joel, precious. Mommy's here. I'm so glad to see you." Of course, it was impossible to move the wall out of the way. The plastic barriers were attached to the ceiling and were protecting Joel from my germs and everyone else's. It was dangerous to expose too much of Joel's body to room air. But I wanted so much to get closer to him—closer to his body—closer to my son who needed me cheering him on, loving him, giving him affection.

Then I opened the boat book and proceeded to show Joel the

different vessels standing up and out of the pages. I moved them up and down on the waves. On each page were also playful fish that showed lots of actions As I turned to the middle page, suddenly a large aircraft carrier seemed to jump off the page at us with a whirlybird helicopter shooting out from the deck and dangling around in the air by a spring. The giggle I heard shot out at me in much the same way. Joel, fascinated with the movement and colors and action so close to him inside the tent, was smiling with his eyes. They sparkled with delight! And his giggle! Such a small thing, something you expect children to do often. But not a child who has been devastated by fire and trapped for weeks in pain within a plastic world. Joel's giggle was a healing thing. It spoke to my concern about his mind and personality to hear him having fun instead of screaming. It seemed to say to me "Joel is still the same Joel."

Despite all the plastic, all the surgeries, all the pain, medication, and dressings, the real Joel was slowly coming back. I had explained previously to Betty, one of Joel's nurses, that I didn't feel Joel had been brain damaged; I thought he was still the same— that he was responding as he had before and that his mind was still as active as before the accident. But it wasn't until I heard him giggle and saw his eyes sparkle that I *knew* it was true.

"Jesus, please heal Joel."
"Bless Joel in the hospital."
"Help Joel not to hurt too much."
Every mealtime, every bedtime, hundreds of children were praying for Joel Sonnenberg. If their parents forgot to pray, the children reminded them. They sent Joel gifts—pictures they had colored, drawings, homemade cards and books, tapes of their young voices—letting Joel know they loved him.
But these children would not have been thinking and praying for Joel if their parents had not first shared their own concern for Joel and his family. Touched by the story of a little boy's struggle for survival and a family's struggle to stay united in the midst of

tragedy, they told their children. As parents they made it a family project to care for Joel and his family—families caring for a family, running with the Sonnenbergs in their race for survival.

Some people said, "Please let us know if there is anything we can do." But it was those who went right ahead and did things, usually without asking, who were truly in the race with this family: people who cared for their needs as persons and as a family unit; people who provided transportation to and from the hospital for Jan; people who gave luggage to replace that lost in the fire; people who saw to it that Mike and Jan received much-needed clothing without having to expend the energy and time to go out and shop for it.

Then there were the friends who gave the gift of laughter by buying Mike a ridiculous blue hat with large brown felt antlers attached to it, so that if he left the hospital but still hadn't found clothes, no one would notice—they'd be absorbed in staring at his hat!

There was the wife of a local seminary faculty member who volunteered to read to Joel.

There were students who brought Mike home-baked pies and cakes and fresh-squeezed apple cider.

And there were the cards—hundreds and hundreds of them— expressions of hope and concern and love. And there were the people who sent money in their cards and letters, through their pastors, through the benevolent funds of various churches. These monetary gifts met urgent needs for decent meals, transportation, the upkeep of two households—one in New York where Jami and her aunt were staying, one in Boston for Mike and Jan.

Best of all, these gifts were given freely and graciously. Those who gave without being asked freed the Sonnenbergs from having to seek the necessities. These people provided things the Sonnenbergs were too busy even to know they needed. Through the loving concern of the Christian community, God provided for their needs as a family more quickly, more efficiently, more thoroughly than any social agency could. "Like a good neighbor, State Farm is there"—but not as quickly as God's people can be. And the Christian community has no red tape, no forms to fill out.

Because their fellow believers supported them in a time of need, the Sonnenbergs did not have to beg for help. Thousands of individuals united to sustain Joel and his family through prayer and practical and financial help.

Mike Sonnenberg was told by the nurses and doctors that he could see Joel as soon as he was strong enough to walk over to the Shriners Burn Institute through a tunnel which connected the two hospitals. So he began walking up and down the hall of the burn unit, painfully increasing the number of trips. He walked and walked.

Because he was doing so much walking, the staff suggested he meet with the psychiatrist. Mike figured they thought he was getting neurotic, overly anxious. He felt trapped. They had him coming and going. If he lay in bed, he was labeled "depressed." If he walked, he was labeled, "anxious." As a result of the interview with the psychiatrist, he was given a tranquilizer. They must have wanted to slow him down, for his first trip over to the Institute was in a wheelchair! Their idea, not his!

The tunnel seemed to go on forever. At last Mike arrived in the large ward. Jan was there and pointed out Joel's tent over on the other side of the room. She helped him don all the plastic garb. He immediately began to sweat profusely under the plastic; he was very hot and his newly grafted hand throbbed.

As he moved closer to the plastic tent, he asked, "How could Joel look worse than at the accident scene?" And there was Joel—spread-eagle, wrapped in white bandages which contrasted with his beet red chest and face. No, he didn't look as grotesque as he had at the accident scene, Mike's last memory of him.

Mike wondered what in the world all the fuss was about his coming over here to see his own son? The staff of the two hospitals had seemed to make such a big deal about it, having him interviewed by the social workers and the psychiatrist, as though everyone had to check him out first.

Thoughts about Joel's present and his future pounded in Mike's brain. He wanted to cry for his son, but he couldn't. The nurses might give him more Valium and restrict his visits. He finally decided nuts to them! He cried.

He told Joel about the Great Pumpkin—it would be Halloween soon. He sang to Joel.

Five minutes after Mike arrived to visit Joel, he was tired. Ten minutes later he was exhausted. In half an hour he felt like he had just run a marathon in a plastic sweat-suit.

When Mike was finally discharged from the hospital, my reactions were mixed. On the surface I was overjoyed that my husband was coming back to me and emerging from "prison," as he called it. So much the outdoorsman, so much in control of himself and his environment, Mike had been incredibly confined in the private isolation room of the burn unit. He emerged severely weakened but bursting with enthusiasm at his release.

Inside, however, I was wondering how in the world I was going to manage caring for him. How was 5-foot, 105 pound Jan Sonnenberg going to cope with her 6-foot, 210 pound husband? He still needed care. For example, daily the bandages covering his open graft areas, where the wounds were not completely closed, needed to be changed. Also, he was still very sore. He was hot one minute, cold the next; his metabolism hadn't straightened itself out yet. Then, too, Mike always pushed himself to the maximum. What was I going to do when he pushed himself too hard? Could I hold him back?

And finally, there was the matter of our togetherness. We were so grateful to be alone together—close, intimate, sharing, without interruption—we cried together. Yet, our first night back together, spent in the large home new friends had graciously opened to us, was a difficult night for me. I was now used to separation from my husband—I had had six weeks of it. I was not used to togetherness. More importantly, my son's race for survival had consumed me totally since September 15th. Now, I had to shift and think not just of Joel's needs and my own immediate survival— food, clothing, housing—but of Mike and his needs. These included intimacy, caring, and loving—and sex with my husband.

Frankly, if I had thought only of my needs at this time, I wouldn't have included sexual relations with my husband as one of them. It was at the bottom of the list. But I had to consider Mike's needs. I loved him, and this was an important physical and emotional way I could care for him. But my emotions and thoughts were so much with Joel—it was as if I were torn in half. As Mike and I made love, the momentum, the strength of it, seemed to me to be violent. Then I thought of Joel as a product of this expression of love and I began to cry.

Mike wondered why was I crying? I explained that I felt miserable because I was not enjoying our physical relationship. But I couldn't separate myself from the hospital where Joel lay in pain, possibly dying.

This struggle for togetherness with separateness was not easily resolved. Ultimately, it was a struggle for the survival of our family unit. If Joel lived, he would need an intact family to help him survive the other crises he would face. Jami needed an intact family. And Mike and I needed each other. The survival of our family unit would hang in the balance long after the life-death issue was settled for our son.

Dick and Suzanne Norwood and their two children lived in a large and beautiful Georgian-style parsonage north of Boston. Dick was a pastor of a Baptist congregation, and he and Suzanne heard about the Sonnenbergs shortly after the accident through the network of prayer. Immediately, they offered to house the Sonnenberg family. The Norwoods had plenty of room in their home so that the guests could have privacy, yet the warm togetherness of the Norwoods when they wanted it. Suzanne was an R.N. with some experience in burns; she soon was helping care for Mike's wounds. Dick was a large man, even taller than Mike, with similar interests—vigorous exercise, outdoor activity, and theological discussions. Their daughter Sonja could be a playmate for Jami when she came up from Nyack. It seemed the perfect residence for the hurting family.

When Dick Norwood visited Joel for the first time, he was amazed at the physical condition of this young child. He thought of his own child, Marguerite, about Joel's age. How would he react if this were his Marguerite? In the course of his ministry, Dick had visited many sick people, some critical. Sometimes he could sense the ones who had given up, who had no fight left; he could see death in their faces. But after being with Joel and praying with him, Dick thought, *This kid has a lot of spunk. I think he just might make it.*

Dick and Suzanne wisely discerned that Mike and Jan needed to be alone to reestablish bonding between them—that their togetherness needed to be fostered. They had been separated during a crucial time; they needed oneness. They noticed Jan's stubborness, the difficulty she had sharing leadership with Mike. The complete independence she had had to muster in the last six weeks was difficult for her to give up. They noticed her lack of caring for Mike's wound on his hand and shoulder because of her total absorption with Joel.

The Norwoods ached for this young couple bearing such a heavy burden. They wanted to help in any way they could. So one evening, Dick lit a fire in the mammoth fireplace of their spacious living room and suggested that Mike and Jan enjoy its warmth on the cold autumn night.

Mike and I had been gazing at the fire together for some time, sitting on the floor before the fireplace. We were exhausted, yet the chill air in the room away from the fire kept us from giving in to our fatigue.

"Honey, I still can't believe this happened to us," I said in despair. "I can't believe Joel was in a fire like that. Eating him away. This all seems like a terrible nightmare. I feel like I'm here but I'm not here."

"We just have to keep remembering that we all could have been burned—all of us could have been dead," Mike said. "I don't believe we made it out alive."

Joel at nine months

Joel at one year, with Mike

Jami and Joel, shortly before the accident—this is the photo Jan hung over Joel's bed in the hospital

The accident scene: car in which Doug Rupp, Mike, and Joel were riding is to the left of the truck in the foreground; car in which Kathy Rupp, Jan, and Jami were riding can be seen crosswise over the tollbooth in the right background

Car in which Jami, Jan, and Kathy were riding

Car in which Joel, Mike, and Doug were riding

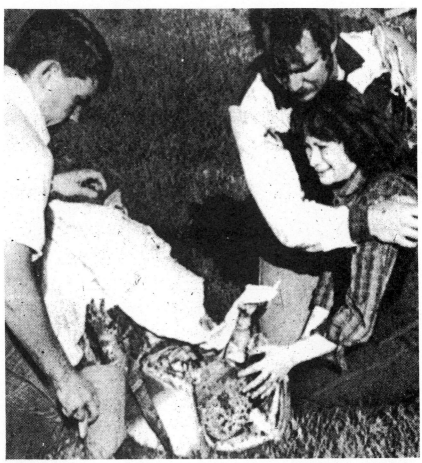

AP photo of accident scene—Mike and Jan are on the right; Joel is in the center

Jan leaves Joel's plastic tent at Shriners Hospital in Boston

Mike and Joel sailing at Camp of the Woods, summer 1980

Jami and Joel in their yard, spring 1980

The Sonnenbergs: Jami, Joel, Mike, Sommer, Jan

Today, Joel climbs jungle gyms . . .

. . . and trees.

"But if we made it, why not Joel? It's not right that he was the only one so hurt—I'd give anything if it had been me instead of Joel," I cried.

"But, honey, can you imagine if I had died and Joel was still burned, too? Or if you and Jami had died and Joel and I were left, both burned? All alone, without you?"

"I get sick just thinking of it—"

"Or Jami burned as bad as Joel. She'd never have made it this far, that's for sure. She's so thin and frail—much weaker."

"Just look at that fire!" I said. "How could anything be so awful? I still can't believe this has happened!"

The crackle of the fire, the high hiss of the wood in front of us seemed suddenly evil. The sounds seemed to echo the ambulance sirens from weeks ago.

"It's scary watching it—I added."

"And it's so destructive. The power of it—the heat of it. Oh, God—I can't watch it, thinking of Joel's body on fire!" Mike put his arm around me as I cried, my face buried in my arm.

"Honey, you just can't imagine how painful a burn is. My hand is killing me. But Joel's going through so much more than that—and those donor sites are excrutiating, and he's having to have them over and over and over—" Mike was crying now.

We lay there in front of the dying fire, our arms around each other. *When are we ever going to stop crying?* was my last thought before we fell asleep.

One morning before Mike and I left the Norwood home for our daily trip to the hospital, I looked at myself in the mirror. Really looked. I needed makeup—badly. My face looked tired, peaked. Lining up the lipstick, mascara, eyeshadow, and blush that my friend Janet had given me right after the accident, I began to wonder, *Will these really make me look more beautiful? Hold it— how can I do this? How can I give attention to my face with all these powders and creams when my son doesn't even have a nor-*

mal face now? I was swamped with guilt. Joel was in the hospital, stripped of his own beautiful skin and tissue; his lips were gone; his lower eyelids had just been replaced by the plastic surgeon; his soft, plump cheeks had been destroyed. As I held the eyelash curler to my eye I was struck by the thought, *Joel no longer even has eyelashes*, and here I was taking time and energy to curl mine and make them look thicker.

I had gone through twenty-eight years, almost twenty-nine, with the face that stared back at me. It had been with me through the major developmental crises of my life such as adolescence. Adolescence, when one pimple meant social devastation. When if the right boy didn't pay enough attention to me, I wanted to die. Those feelings seemed remote now, but at the time were very intense. Then there was young adulthood, when my goals were a career and marriage. I remembered my first date with Mike—a blind date while still in college, arranged by his sister Nancy.

"Hey, Mike," she had told him. "There's a real spitfire I think you'd like who plays on our intermural volleyball team."

But what if I had been burned? What would Nancy have said about me then to Mike? Would I have even been considered as a blind date for Mike if my face had been damaged as Joel's was?

I threw the eyelash curler down. Its metallic bounce seemed to ask, *Why weren't you burned instead of Joel?* Indeed, why hadn't I been defaced, stripped of most of my skin and tissue, instead of Joel? Only twenty-two months old, with all those major developmental crises yet to go through—and with what kind of face? It would have been so much easier for me, I thought, to have been burned instead of my son. I sobbed, angry that I had not been burned instead of him—guilt-ridden that I would take the time to put make-up on my normal, unburned face when my son didn't have much of a face left. It was many days before I attempted to apply the make-up again.

For Joel's appearance was something we were grappling with now. He was still wrapped in bandages, but slowly they were being removed from his face. Were we prepared for his facial appearance? Joel, black and charred, was one sight; Joel completely bandaged was another. And Joel covered with grafted skin was yet another. Skin did not replace subcutaneous fat and muscle that had been burned off, the padding that provides shape and form for the "upholstery" of the face and body. I was, indeed, frightened of seeing my son's face without the padding. What could it possibly look like?

I asked one of the nurses, "What do these kids look like after a burn like this?" I wished someone could show me some pictures just to help prepare me for Joel's face. Her reply was: "Just look over there on the other side of the room if you can stomach it. See that little boy? He had a very deep burn on his body and face."

I looked. It was a gruesome sight. It made me sick. Joel look like that? No! It couldn't be. I looked away. I looked back again. I looked again and again in the days ahead. I saw this same little boy kicking balls around—smiling, laughing, having a great time despite all his limitations. This child wasn't so gruesome! His spirit was enviable! Downright admirable! He had spunk—personality. He was vibrant.

"He cute," I said to the same nurse several days later.

"But Joel's burns are even deeper on his face and head," the nurse replied, trying to help me comprehend what lay ahead.

I began to think of a new race ahead of us. If Joel did survive this race for survival, we would be starting a new one—the race to restore Joel's appearance would take the very best plastic surgeons in the world, and he was going to have them if I had anything to do about it. Yes, we would press on, running until the very best was done for Joel.

After we learned that Joel's eyesight remained intact, our next urgent concern was that his fingers and toes be saved. We worried about the handicap that loss of fingers and their manipulative capacity would represent. Without his fingers, how could Joel open a door, pound with his hammer, feed himself? The toes were vitally important, too. Lost fingers could never be replaced, but sometimes toes can be "transplanted" to function as fingers. In addition, toes—especially the big and little toes—are important for balance.

How could Joel walk, run, and hike without them? So we were especially concerned about these digits.

"What is your opinion regarding Joel's fingers and toes," I asked one of the nurses. "Do you think he'll have any?"

Previously, when I had asked others that question, I had been told, "We just have to wait and see." But this nurse was frank.

"No way," the nurse replied. "His fingers are charred and his toes are very bad. I don't think there will be any left." His honesty shocked me, but I respected his truthful opinion.

Still, the answer scared me. We had to prevent this loss. I kept asking people to pray specifically for Joel's fingers and toes. Fingers and toes. What would Joel's life be without them? We urged people to pray that his precious fingers and toes be saved. Joel's life, of course, still hung in the balance; but if he lived, those fingers and toes were important for his return to a normal life.

Toward the middle of October, despite our prayers, Joel's fingers began to fall off. During the dressing changes the nurses would find the charred pieces that had simply been too damaged to survive. Joel was losing his precious, irreplacable fingers, one by one.

Each time I learned he had lost another finger, I panicked. All the prayers in the world weren't stopping this loss! In desperation I called the pastor of a Presbyterian church who had suggested three weeks earlier that he and the elders of his church come and anoint Joel's head with oil and pray for healing. I had shied away from the idea at the time. I knew it would be difficult to get permission to do this because of the need to protect Joel against bacteria. Then, too, I felt we would be reaching out for the impossible. Although I knew that anointing for healing was biblical, it represented an extreme act of healing simply not possible for Joel.

Now, facing the loss of Joel's fingers, I asked the pastor to come with his elders to anoint Joel. *Why not?* I asked myself. *What is there to lose?* And I did believe God could keep the rest of Joel's fingers intact if He chose to.

They came—young men and old. I was impressed by their great faith and their concern for my son. We went up to the unit together, where they touched the top of Joel's bandaged head with the oil they had brought. Just a little oil on their gloved fingers, but it represented faith and hope for Joel, for his body. Healing, promise, power—in the midst of our powerlessness.

But this power was to show itself in ways other than the saving of Joel's fingers and toes. Joel lost them all, one by one. His left hand was so deeply burned that it had to be removed.

November

Back home in Nyack, New York, Jami Sonnenberg played and fought with her cousin B.J. and with her neighborhood friends. Many opened their homes to Jami, her Aunt Nancy, and B.J., inviting them to dinner. Family and community were offering Jami their love and support, but emotional healing would take time. The accident haunted Jami's memory.

When Jami and her friend Johnny played cars and trucks, Jami would bang the cars together and then have Johnny's toy fire trucks come to put out the fire.

Often at mealtimes, Jami prayed, "Dear God, thank You that when Jesus comes our faces, our arms, everything, will be perfect again," and "Thank You for Joel—he is so beautiful."

Despite her strong and simple faith, Jami's sorrows sometimes overwhelmed her. She missed her family. No one could take their place. She told her Aunt Nancy, "When I think about daddy and mommy and Joel, I just have to cry." And she did.

Although we had decided it was best for Jami to stay at our home in Nyack, it was hard being separated from our precious daughter. We were missing important days in Jami's young life. More than that, we were missing a part of our family, a part of ourselves.

One of the best gifts we received during those early weeks were letters from Jami's nursery-school teacher. She wrote to me every week and gave a detailed day-to-day account of Jami's life at school. The letters helped us feel close to Jami and reassured us that home was the best place for her at this time. We cried when we read the first letter:

Dear Mrs. Sonnenberg,

Since Friday was Jami's first day back at school, I thought you would like to hear how everything went. Well, it went just fine.

She seemed happy, and she fit right into the group again naturally. Every day when I have been calling roll and talking about who is absent, I have mentioned Jami, so the children in the group would not forget her. . . .

While we were at snack time, sitting around together, Jami described the entire accident to me in some detail. I was filled with admiration and respect for you and for the people who were caring for Jami. It is because you have been open with her that she is able to be open. It is so much better for her to be able to talk about it than to have it shut away inside her. I feel you have done beautifully by her and I can't begin to tell you how much I admire your sensitivity and perception and understanding of how to help her recover from this experience.

We cried because we needed to hear this.

On November 1, Jami turned four. Mike and I decided we must go home to Nyack for her birthday; it was an important time for Jami, and we should be with her. I will never forget that first time Mike and Jami and I were back together in our own home—without Joel.

As we unlocked the front door and stepped into the hallway, it felt so good to be home. But as I climbed the steep stairwell to the bedrooms, I imagined Joel at the top of the stairs with his arms outstretched as he often had been in the past, his beautiful smile and his bouncing body waiting expectantly to be carried down the steps. I couldn't wait to reach him and hug him to me. But, of course, the stairs were empty.

I went into his room. His crib was there. His toys were there. But he was not. I sobbed, scared that he would never come back to his room and to my arms.

As I walked around the house, the rooms seemed full of voices of the past. Voices laughing, yelling, giggling, even fighting. I missed the voices, I missed the activity, even the fighting. Would we ever be back here together in our home?

It was unbelievably painful not to have Joel with us after supper.

This was the time when the kids always roughhoused with Mike and we did things together as a family—read stories, popped popcorn, played games, showed home movies, or played the player piano.

Later that night as I lay in bed I strained to listen for Joel's cry from his room, signaling that he was awake and needed attention. Wishful thinking. He was not there. Instead, his face loomed before me as I closed my eyes to try to sleep. I was glad to be back in my own bed, in my own home; I was overwhelmed by the friends who had called, reaching out to us with help and care. But I was also exhausted with grief—with the stark reality that hit me anew, that though we were back in our own home it was not the same, and it didn't seem that our life would ever be normal again.

In the middle of the night I woke sobbing, chocking back moans so as not to wake up Mike. The bed started shaking just from my spasms of grief. Mike woke up. He hugged me as he always did when I was sobbing. We cried together. It helped to cry together. We did a lot of it.

Mike lost a lot of sleep in those early months because I was always waking up in the middle of the night, unable to sleep, and would start crying about Joel. Sometimes the pressure to keep racing, to keep cheering Joel on and all the surrounding events crowded out the time, energy, and apparent need to cry. But some nights, in dreams, I relived the horror of our accident or of Joel's plight in the hospital. In my dreams I would be choking, exploding with emotional pain, crying hysterically. Then I would wake up sobbing. These dreams were my release valve during the pressurized days of waiting.

Because my time with Jami was brief and her needs special, I wrote her this birthday letter to leave with her—a gift she might need even more in days to come than her birthday presents.

Dear Jami,
    Your fourth birthday has come and found our life different than we could ever have imagined. It was so hard for me to leave the

hospital where Joel was still hovering between life and death. But I knew I must because Halloween is always a fun time for you, and the next day is your birthday.

I must admit I didn't feel like celebrating at all. I love you very much, but I am torn between your needs and your brother's needs. Joel's needs are very great right now. My need as a mother is to do all I can for my children. . . .

Joel may die eventually. I am afraid this may happen when I am not there, or maybe because I am there. Still, life has to go on for you—and you will remember your fourth birthday party for the rest of your life. If Joel survives this, what will he—not even two years old—remember of his mother's not being there for four or five days?

I contacted friends who helped us celebrate your birthday in style with a grand party. One friend decorated with balloons, another made a grand cake just like you wanted. "A lion cake, mommy," you said, "just like Jacquelyn had at her party." And a lion cake you had. Another friend planned games complete with prizes. Another made you a special Halloween costume, "a fairy princess," just what you wanted. I don't know what I would have done without these friends. I do know one thing—I don't have the energy to do all that they are doing for me and for you. I even had to give a list of presents to buy for you to a friend.

But there was one present I bought for you myself three weeks ago. I had to buy it when I saw it in the children's department of a large department store in Boston. A beautiful doll with dark brown hair, pigtails, saucer eyes. She looks just like you. When I saw her, I knew you had to have her. And that you would love her. "Jami" you quickly named her. And then later when she rode with you on the airplane to grandma's, she became "Jet Jami." I'll never forget your surprise and delight when you opened the box— your first real doll.

It has been a difficult two months for you. You have been shuttled back and forth, back and forth. First you stayed with the MacKenzies, and then at home with Aunt Nancy.

Jami, I have missed you very much. Before Aunt Nancy took you to New York I hugged and hugged you. Remember? You didn't want me to stop. And I didn't want to stop. So we hugged and hugged each other, saying good-by for a while. For how long? We didn't know. You cried and cried that night—missing us.

We were thrilled that we could be with you again. We don't know when we will all be in our home again. . . .

But I do know one thing. I'm proud to have you as a daughter—now four years old. You have had to deal with more grief and tears and terror than many, many people. And still it isn't over. I can't tell of my gratitude that you were not burned. You are so fragile. I don't think you could have taken the physical assault of the burn as your brother has. But I am amazed and thrilled that you are coping with the emotional trauma of this horrendous experience. You, too, are a survivor in this great race we are running—together.

I returned to Boston the day after Jami's birthday. Mike stayed behind to attend to some business but would follow on a later flight.

As I entered Joel's ward at Shriners, I immediately noticed that one of the four plastic units was empty. For days that unit had been the center of urgent activity; the little boy lying inside it had been very sick. His burns had healed long ago, but his lungs were acutely infected and he was slowly suffocating. Now he had died—after spending months in the unit.

I was disgusted when I learned that he was kept in the house of plastic up to the very end of his life. He was not allowed out of that plastic cocoon even when he was dying. The germs, the nurses explained, were too dangerous and could prove fatal to the other children. Again I asked myself, *if Joel dies, how will he die?* Will he be pounded into further and faster unconsciousness by someone trying to revive him? Will they be sticking even more tubes in him? Will hordes of doctors and nurses be running around, frantically working on him?

The death of this young boy made me ask again—*how do I want my son to die?* I certainly wanted his death to be peaceful. I wanted to hold him and rock him and love him right up to the end. And I wanted to tear down the plastic walls and throw them out the window!

I was frightened by my lack of control over Joel's treatment, especially over the way his dying would be handled. When could we as parents draw the line and say, "Now the spiritual dimension is the most important to Joel"? We felt that our wishes about how Joel should die had been taken out of our hands and that no one cared what we wanted. Frankly, this was infuriating. We felt like screaming, "This is the only earthly life our son will have. If he is going to die—it will be the only time he dies. If our child dies, we are going to be there—and anyone who comes between us and our son will be sorry." To us, how our son would die was just as important as motivating him to live.

But we didn't scream. In fact, we didn't discuss this issue with the staff at all because we were so afraid that our wishes would not be respected.

This young boy's death also made me realize anew the urgency of the race of survival for those remaining. Who would be next? Would any of these kids make it.

"Joel,—hang on!" I wanted to scream.

But as Christians, Mike and I struggled with a higher question. With renewed determination to keep running for survival came awareness of the spiritual race whose goal is eternity. Eternal being. Life everlasting. The greatest promise ever. Were we also preparing our son for this?

For indeed, it was possible we would not win this earthly race for life. And losers got death. But for Christians death also held a promise—life forever in heaven. Were we preparing our son for both alternatives? How did we go about preparing Joel for heaven? And at the same time cheer him on for life? Life was temporary compared to eternity in heaven, but we desperately wanted this temporary life for our son. Death and heaven, it seemed to us, had to be thought of optimistically and realistically. To be at peace with death meant to be a peace with life.

We began talking about heaven more often with Joel. We sang and played songs for him which were optimistic about heaven and how great it was.

> Jesus, I heard you had a big house
> Where I'd have a room of my own
> And Jesus, I heard you had a big yard
> Big enough to let a kid roam.

I heard you had clothes in your closet
  Just the right size that I wear
And Jesus, I heard if I give you my heart
  That you would let me go there.
Jesus, I heard about meal time
  That all of your children come to eat
I heard you had a great big table
  Where every kid could have a seat.
Jesus, I heard there'd be plenty
  Of good things for children to share
And Jesus, I just want to tell you
  I sure would like to go there. . . .
Jesus, I heard that in your big house
  There's plenty of love to go round
I heard there's always singing and laughter
  To fill the place with happy sounds.
And I've been thinking' 'bout a Friend
  Who'd want to give me all that He's got
Before, I just have to thank him, for
  He sure must love me a lot. . . .
Yes, He sure must love me a lot.

We wanted Joel to know that heaven meant an end to pain, disability, and confinement—that it meant wholeness and happiness, laughter and singing. That it is a place where promises are fulfilled.

But Joel's burn was deeper than any of us ever dreamed possible!

I was waiting down in the lobby of the hospital, waiting for Mike to return from a trip to New York and for Joel to return from surgery. They were taking a look at his head today. The nurses had kept saying, "The burn is very deep on his head." I didn't register that as anything more drastic than we'd already seen. But I was on pins and needles. When would it ever be over? What were they doing? What were they finding?

Suddenly, the doctors were in front of me—the residents and the hospital chief of staff.

"Is your husband here yet?" the chief of staff asked, looking very grave.

"No, but I expect him back this evening."

"I was hoping to tell you this news when he was with you."

"Bad news?" I felt punched in the stomach.

"Your son has a very extensive and deep skull burn like we have never seen before on a living person. It covers the entire top of his skull and down the sides; the size is as if you placed a bowl on top of his head . . . that's how deep and severe your child's burn is on his head."

I was shocked—horrified—chilled. Stabbed in the chest. I placed my hand on top of my head as if to hold myself together, to hold onto my sanity. Just then the senior resident walked away from us—through the lobby—out the doors. He sat on the front steps of the hospital.

"What do you do for something like this?" I implored. "Put a metal plate on his head instead of his skull? On this wide an area? What happens when he grows?"

"This is all new to us," the chief of staff answered. "We are a pioneering, research facility. We have done things in this hospital in the last two years, saved lives of children, thought impossible before. But we don't have all the answers. I sure wish we did. I wish I had the answers to your questions—"

I was crying hard now, and he put his arm around me. I sobbed, "Joel—is so strong—oh, God—what happens now?"

I appreciated this world-renowned surgeon's honesty and strength to say, "We don't know." Here was a powerful man admitting his lack of power.

But I was crushed by the severity of Joel's injury. My dear, dear son. So strong—so brave. He had endured so much. I was so proud of him at that moment. Frankly, I thought I could press on in any race for Joel. But to compete against this new unknown, this extensive injury to the vital bone protecting my son's brain, his mind, his personality, his bodily functions. This was the greatest threat to my whole drive for Joel, for it threatened the commitment I had made to God that Joel's mind would not be touched.

Joel's life seemed to be in renewed danger now. So was my commitment.

As Jan was dealing with the news of Joel's skull injury, Mike was enroute to Boston. The weekend he had just spent in Nyack had been a reaffirmation of the network of faith and support provided by the family of God.

On Saturday night, the young couples' fellowship of their church—a group Mike and Jan belonged to—had sponsored a dinner to raise money to replace the car the Sonnenbergs had lost in the accident. The response was overwhelming. So many people flocked into the church that it seemed there wouldn't be room in the large church basement hall to hold them all. Soon thousands of dollars filled the large cardboard donation box decorated to look like a car.

Then, to everyone's surprise and amazement, Mike Sonnenberg walked in. The place went wild, everyone standing to clap and cheer him on. Mike felt like he was back on the football field at college and had just completed a spectacular play.

When the clapping, cheering, and greeting had subsided, Mike began to speak, explaining what being in the hospital had been like and telling them about Joel. He described Joel's condition and a typical day for Joel in the hospital. He told them about life for Jan and Jami and himself and about adjusting to Boston. He knew it would help this network of supporting friends to visualize what was happening in the race for Joel's life so that they could pray more specifically.

On Sunday, Mike spoke in church, in the same sanctuary where, weeks earlier, the congregation had begun to pray for Joel and his family. Mike thanked the church again for their support, for their gifts of money and of prayer. After church he was mobbed by well-wishers who wanted to shake his hand or pat him on the back.

Joel would celebrate his second birthday on Thanksgiving in his plastic house. That his birthday, November 22, coincided with this national day of thanksgiving hardly seemed accidental—we were very thankful Joel was still alive.

But the plastic house and all it symbolized was with us, too. Only a week before we had learned the extent of Joel's skull injury. Since then we had become increasingly depressed and defeated. I was weighed down with a real, ever-present fear: despite the promises of God and of Joel's own strength and potential, I had a strong feeling that Joel was not going to make it.

So, in one sense, I really didn't want to celebrate his birthday because I was afraid it would be his last. I couldn't bear that thought. But the celebration seemed to spur Mike on; he even took movies. No balloons, candles, or cake were allowed inside Joel's tent, but there were many presents.

These presents had been a source of anxiety. What could we give him? What could an injured child play with inside a plastic tent? More important, if he survived and got out of that tent, what toys could he use? Soft or fluffy toys couldn't be included because they would harbor germs. When I was home for Jami's birthday, I had gone up into the attic of our house and looked at the toys stored there—presents I had bought at summer toy sales and packed away, anticipating the fun Joel would have with them. A large plastic dump truck, a bulldozer, a crane. Toys Joel would have loved—before the accident. Would he ever be able to use them now? Without fingers? Without a hand?

But Joel's birthday was an occasion for celebration. As we opened his presents for him—cassette tapes with matching story-books, simple pop-up toys, wooden blocks—we heard his gleeful laugh again. And as an extra-special birthday surprise we actually got to kiss Joel, skin to skin, without the plastic layers.

On Thanksgiving Day the hospital cook, Arthur, shared his holiday spirit with the patients, parents, and staff by preparing a fantastic feast. The pies alone were a real meal! Mike savored them all, pumpkin, mince, *and* apple. Of course there was also a huge turkey, dressing, sweet potatoes, vegetables, salads, and rolls.

At least eight parents were there to eat this Thanksgiving banquet, and as Mike and I and the others sat down at the table prepared by the hospital cook and his staff, I mentally sang a familiar Thanksgiving hymn:

> We gather together to ask the Lord's blessing,
> He chastens and hastens his will to make known;
> The wicked oppressing now cease from distressing,
> Sing praises to His name, He forgets not His own.

Giving thanks. Thanks-giving. Bounty. Food. Closeness. Family, Joel's birthday.

The week before Thanksgiving, Mike, Jami and I had taken a short trip south of Boston to visit Plymouth Plantation where the Pilgrims had lived in primitive grass huts along the bay of Massachusetts. Simple living. Simply survival. Yet those people had given thanks for all they had. Now as we sat down for our Thanksgiving meal, I reflected on those courageous people in a new, forbidding land with few possessions. Weren't we a lot like those early Pilgrims?

By now we were quite familiar with Boston, but still it was not our own city. We had had to leave everything familiar—job, home, family, church, school. The residence where we were living belonged to someone else. Indeed, the very clothes we were wearing had been purchased by someone else. The luggage we now owned to carry the clothing in had been given to us. The car we were driving had been loaned to us by my parents. Our needs were being met by the use of money sent to us by various individuals, organizations, and churches. The hospital where Joel was being cared for was a free gift to us, provided by the generosity of the Shrine of North America. Even the food we ate today was a gift of the hospital.

Like the Pilgrims, we had been stripped down to the very essence of life-survival. Yet everything was provided for us abundantly and, in many instances, before we even knew there was a need.

The network was still expanding, as evidenced by messages the Sonnenbergs continued to receive from across the country.

A congregation in Oregon sent a packet of prayer cards every week. The parishioners filled the cards out during their church services and placed them in the offering plates. On the cards were written personal messages of encouragement.

The Sonnenbergs heard from Sunday school classes, women's groups, youth groups, and individual pastors.

In Kentucky, one Pentecostal church of 4,000 members knelt and prayed for Joel.

Mennonite churches in Ohio and Indiana prayed and sent money.

In Maine and Massachusetts, Catholic priests reminded their parishioners to pray.

Many women who didn't know Jan sent messages because, as mothers, they felt a special bond with her as they thought of Joel and of their own children.

The boundaries of the United States could not circumscribe the growing concern for Joel. Many of Mike and Jan's friends knew missionaries overseas and sent the word out to them to pray. Messages began to come from Indonesia, Australia, Canada, Mexico, Saudi Arabia, India, Japan, the Philippines, Germany, Scandanavia—even from the bush country of Upper Volta, West Africa. Soon the candles mutiplied to become a powerful flame of prayer for the little boy still precariously balanced between life and death in a Boston hospital.

December

December! I had been dreading this month. Christmas—joy, happiness, presents. It had been three months and still Joel's life hung in the balance.

Nancy MacKenzie sensed that I needed to get in the holiday spirit for the sake of the rest of my family—Mike and Jami—so she invited us up to her home in New Hampshire for a weekend away from the hospital several weeks before Christmas. Nancy had already decorated her house, made Christmas cookies, was playing Christmas music, and had presents for us all. That weekend there was even a small parade in her town complete with Santa Claus.

Saturday evening, after putting Jami to bed, I sat alone in a rocking chair in front of the fireplace. Mike was in the other room watching television with Nancy and her husband, Alex.

As I rocked back and forth, listening to the Christmas music on Nancy's stereo, I thought about our drive up to New Hampshire the day before. As we had neared the southern New Hampshire border on the northern Massachusetts highway, we were traveling the same asphalt that we had traveled back on September 15.

Mike had said, "I'd really like to take a look at the accident site again, Jan. I'd like to get an overview of the scene and maybe try to figure out what happened and why there at the tollbooths."

Yes, it seemed like the right time, now almost three months later, to start trying to fit the pieces of the puzzle together. What had really happened? Why did a tractor-trailer plow into an idling string of cars in the extreme right-hand lane of a toll plaza?

As we approached the tollbooths, they were clearly visible way down the road, sitting on a wide-open expanse of flat earth and asphalt. Within a mile or so of the tollbooths, we passed a sign: "Toll plaza ahead." Hadn't the driver of the truck seen this sign? Was this road new to him? Was he high on drugs? Or asleep at the wheel? What could have been going through the man's mind?

As we neared the far right booth, I could barely concentrate on the sights: my heart pounded loud in my ears as I wheeled around to check out the vehicles approaching us from the rear.

Mike shouted, "Look at the top of the tollbooth! It's still scorched black from the flames!"

But the road held no skid marks, the grass no smoldering remains of bodies on fire. The guardrail was no longer bent; even that mark of the accident had been replaced with new materials to cover up evidences of destruction.

We glided through the toll easily, and looking back, Mike suggested, "I want to go up on the overpass that overlooks the entire scene to get a broader overview."

As Mike stopped the car on the overpass bridge and we looked down on the accident site, we were immediately impressed with the open, unchaotic expanse of the area. Many tollbooth areas are very congested and narrow, but this one seemed so atypical. It even seemed peaceful. All the booths were clearly visible way down the road. Furthermore, there was a grassy field to the right of the booth where we had been rear-ended. Why didn't the driver of the truck head for that grassy area? That is certainly what we would have done had we lost our brakes. We would have tried to avoid hitting the cars. And certainly he didn't apply his brakes for the first time only seventy feet from the toll area when he was hauling thirty-six tons!

WHAT HAD HAPPENED HERE? OUR SON WAS STILL LYING IN A HOSPITAL BED AFTER THREE MONTHS BECAUSE OF THE IMPACT OF A TRACTOR-TRAILER. AN INNOCENT BABY WAS SUFFERING BECAUSE OF SOME JERK? A man who desired to cause destruction? Could this be? A man who forgot to check his brakes? Or who didn't apply the brakes at all? My impression after viewing the accident site was one of profound shock. It seemed there was no other way to interpret the accident than as the result of a deliberate, aggressive, violent act. Either that or extreme negligence.

As I continued to rock in Nancy's chair by the fireplace, I once more picked up the newspaper clipping that Nancy had saved for me to read.

HAMPTON CRASH YIELDS CHARGE

HAMPTON—A trucker from Nova Scotia was scheduled to be arraigned in Hampton District Court this morning on a charge of aggravated assault in connection with a fiery chain-reaction accident at the Hampton tollbooth Saturday afternoon that sent nine people to area hospitals.

[The truck driver] was arrested and held in lieu of $25,000 cash bail after his tractor-trailer truck slammed into a row of passenger cars waiting to pay tolls at the I-95 interchange.

The driver said the brakes on the truck failed just before the truck struck the rear of an auto driven by _____ of North Andover, Mass.

State Police Sgt. Sheldon P. Sullivan said _____ was held pending a determination if the brakes indeed failed. State police impounded the vehicles in the crash and were to inspect the autos today.

Four persons remain hospitalized this morning. Most seriously injured was 18-month-old Joel Sonnenberg of South Nyack, N.Y., who was listed in poor condition at a Boston hospital with burns over 75 percent of his body.

Two of the autos involved in the accident caught fire on impact.

"It looked like a battle scene," said a motorist who arrived after the accident. "Two cars were charred, another was sliced in half."

A Hampton firefighter said "two cars burst into flames after the truck smashed into them."

The accident tangled northbound traffic on the heavily used interstate for hours, police said.

Foster's Daily Democrat, Dover, N.H.
Monday Evening, September 17, 1979

Then a lullaby began on Nancy's stereo—about a young infant, a boy, our Savior, rocked to sleep by his mother. I was overwhelmed. Jesus. Prince, Counselor. Friend. The Timeless One had taken on Time in the form of an infant boy. Had taken on pain, suffering, anguish, grief. Yet He was also a son of an earthly mother. I thought of Mary, of her joy and her sorrow. Was there meaning here for me? My son's body seemed to have been sacrificed for some higher purpose which was God's—certainly not mine. What mission did He have for Joel? I thought of all the people who had spoken of a purpose in Joel's suffering.

"God's hand is in all this, I can sense it," stated one minister. My mother's words came back to me, "God will turn this around for good—you wait and see." My friend Barb's encouragement, "Your family has been chosen—special—set apart. Who knows what is to become of this? You are God's chosen family to endure this. I couldn't do this—my family could never handle this. But God just knew you could do it."

Mary was in my mind, rocking her child to sleep—peaceful, contented sleep just as I had rocked Joel before our accident. Did Mary sense the pain and anguish of the years ahead? Did she have any idea of what was coming? The angel had told her that she had been chosen, that she would bear the Savior, that He would be great. But the angel had never spoken of suffering. The angel had borne glad tidings of great joy to all people.

I could remember our joy when Joel was born. Since our first child had been a girl, I wanted a boy for Mile. Like most men, Mike never really said, "Yes, I want a boy." Instead he said, "As long as it's healthy it doesn't matter." But I knew that it did matter to Mike, deep inside. I wanted a son for Mike, and I was sure that the baby I was carrying was a boy.

Even Jami seemed to be thinking "boy." When we took her to the five-and-dime store to pick out a present for the new baby shortly-to-be-born, we allowed her complete freedom to chose any toy her two-year-old mind thought best. After romping down the aisles, without any coaching from us, she had picked out—a blue football! Mike was ecstatic!

Mike's first words to me about his son were an excited, "Honey, he's got my thighs!" I could tell he was already planning things he and Joel would do together. His son would be special to him in a way I could never really understand as a woman.

One look at our newborn son, and I knew he was destined for great things—just like his father. His muscles—large and defined, his broad little shoulders, his long fingers. Joel was all Sonnenberg.

Where was that destiny now? What had happened to all that promise? How could we give Joel an active, useful, highly valued life? If God had a purpose in our pain, in his pain, what was it?

As these questions tore through me, I recalled the past summer. It had been the summer of the seventeen-year locusts, or "cicadas" as Mike insisted on calling them. These large insects were everywhere. The kids enjoyed watching them, and with their childish wonder came an interest in the metamorphosis that was taking place in these creatures. One day they were in the ground as hard-cased larvae in our sandbox. Several days later they were flying insects, finally shedding their "skin" as they clung to tree trunks or branches, eating, munching, nibbling, everywhere they went.

One day I found Jami at our side door. "Mommy . . . mommy . . . look, look . . . I have a bug on my shoulder. He's so-o-o friendly!" It was a large, red-eyed cicada, very ugly by any non-insect-lover's standard, but Jami was fascinated by the creatures of change as her young mind tried to grasp what was taking place in our yard.

As the cicada's hum seemed to drone everywhere that summer, other changes were taking place, too.

A young mother, whose parents lived in our neighborhood, died and left three young children. Though I did not personally know this woman, I was shaken. I felt so terrible for her children, to have to continue life without their mother—how would this affect them in years to come? Innocent children. I began to wonder if my children might have to live without me someday—maybe soon. Who knew—I could be next! Could they possibly survive without me? Then, more significantly, the fearful question: could I survive without them? This haunted me. What would I do if something happened to my kids? To one? To both? What would it be like, after having a beautiful child for a few years, suddenly not to have them anymore? What would it be like to see pictures on the walls that included two children, when only one was left? How would I explain this to the other child?

"Here is your brother/sister who was once your very best friend. But now he/she is in heaven. Someday you will see them again, but for right now a picture is all we have to remember him/her by."

How would this affect the other child? How would it affect me? Would I live through it?

I began to dream about this fear. I was in the maple tree in our yard. The children were there with me in the branches. Suddenly a violent flood came, sweeping away all in its path. We clung to the tree as hard as we could. But, finally, one child was swept away. What should I do? Should I stay in the tree with the other child, assuring that child's safety, or should I jump in to save the lost one, even though it was truly impossible? I jumped into the churning water. I had to. I couldn't bear not trying to retrieve the child I had lost. I woke up sobbing hysterically.

Could I really live through a tragedy affecting my child? This question haunted me all summer. Finally one morning, walking down our stairwell while doing household chores, I began thinking about living without one or both of my children, or without my husband, and I started crying as if it were really happening to me.

Now, on this December night in New Hampshire my mind flashed back to reality. I was still rocking, staring into the fire, and that which I had feared this past summer had come to pass. A tragedy indeed had befallen us. One of my children had been severely injured; his survival was still questionable. Yet here I was, alive. I hadn't lost my sanity or my grip on life. Mike and Jami were alive and well. We had survived so far.

It became clear to me on that wintry evening, watching and listening to the hiss and crackle of the dancing flames before me, that God had kept His promise. He was faithful. He had remained the same—unchanged. Always there. Steady, secure. In control of our situation though we were not. Just as He had spoken to a great leader long ago through a burning bush to indicate His Presence, so here through these flames He reminded me of His declaration to Moses: "I AM." "I am with you always." "I never change."

After all this suffering, I was still afraid Joel would die. I still didn't think I could bear the death of my son. Yet, in these quiet moments with the holiday season fast approaching, God was reminding and reassuring, "I AM." No matter what the outcome of this great race, His promise would hold fast.

Mike and Jan decided to take Jami back to Nyack to have Christmas in their own home. They arrived there three days before the holiday. They had been home only two hours when the presents started to trickle in.

One woman heard from a storekeeper in Nyack that the Sonnenbergs had stopped by his store window and greatly admired her handcrafted ceramic crèche. She made another set just for them.

A women from Mike and Jan's church fashioned hand-sewn Raggedy Ann and Andy dolls for Jami and Joel.

A young couple from the Sonnenberg's church dropped off presents for Mike and Jan, personal jewelry and tasteful clothing for Mike.

Several professors' wives brought over homemade Christmas cookies.

Friends invited them over for Christmas dinner so that Jan wouldn't have to cook an elaborate meal.

Kathy and Doug Rupp drove from Ohio so that Mike and Jan would have relatives with them for this first Christmas since their accident.

Finally, after almost three months of praying for Joel Sonnenberg, one particular child was bored with it all. It was 8:00 P.M. Time for bed. Dick Norwood and his daughter Sonja knelt by her bed, as they did every evening, for prayers. Sometimes Sonja said profound things that surprised Dick. Tonight was no exception.

"Jesus," she implored, "please, please, make up Your mind what You are going to do with Joel—I'm so *tired* of praying for him. . . ."

Two days later, after surgery on the back of his head, Joel emerged from his plastic unit! He was never placed back in it.

We were elated! He was in a regular hospital bed at last. Out of plastic! It was as if someone had said to us, "He's going to live. Joel is going to live." Joel had survived! Our son had survived one of the worst burns this burn institution had ever seen!

Now we could touch him . . . hold him . . . love him . . . without the barrier. Soon we were able to play with him more actively. It was such a thrill to pick him up and carry him around the ward. We couldn't get enough of him.

But now we faced a new phase of Joel's injury—rehabilitation. This involved motivating Joel to walk and eat. It involved functioning. Trying to mobilize Joel to the highest level of functioning possible. As this phase began, however, Mike and I had some difficult orientation as we were reintroduced to Joel's body—reacquainted with the total appearance of our son.

Before the exercise periods when we would try to encourage Joel to walk, the nurse would unwrap the gauze which held Joel's heavy splints onto his legs. How skinny his legs looked, even with the heavy elastic ace bandages wound around them. If his legs were that skinny with a covering over them, what were they like with the bandages off? I was afraid to look. Sometimes I would sneak a peak at the little boy lying in the bed next to Joel. It was easier for me to look at another child's body than to see the reality of my own son's.

When by chance one day the nurses unwound the gauze around his splints and the ace bandages in my presence, I gasped at the appearance of Joel's legs. They looked like toothpicks! Toothpicks! It looked as though his skin, so carefully grafted, had been stretched over bare bones. I was sick! How could these puny sticks even support his weight, let alone propel him forward to walk?

My desire to be more directly involved in Joel's physical care led me to ask the nurse, "Could I help give Joel a tub bath?"

"Of course," was her reply.

I was thrilled to be permitted to do this. But I was not prepared for the shock of seeing the totality of Joel's body covered with mesh grafts. This was the first time I had seen my son's new body all at once. His skin was no longer smooth, softly rounded with baby fat. It was no longer the black body I had seen at the scene of the accident, of course. It was the body that was left under the bandages—the body Joel had been alive in for months—but I was seeing it for the first time completely uncovered. It looked so red, like fire itself, and so sore. Newly meshed grafts are always very red for months. The grafted skin was bumpy, but evenly so. Frankly, all I could think of was that his body now appeared to be covered with skin like a reptile's, for the evenly patterned grafts resembled scales.

These grafts saved Joel's life, I kept repeating to myself. But I was horrified. What kind of a life would my child have with a body like this? Could he ever go out in public?

The 8" × 10" portrait of Joel and Jami flashed into my mind. When Joel was moved to the Shriners Burn Institute I posted that same portrait at the foot of his plastic unit. It had stayed there for months and months. Joel—beautiful, fresh, sparkling-faced Joel.

No—the picture was no longer Joel. Joel was here screaming in the bathtub of water with a new body. A body that didn't even look human—let alone like Joel. *Oh, Joel,* I mentally moaned as I sponged him down with water, gulping back the tears, *what has happened to you?* Of course I had known that Joel's body would bear the marks of the burn. But like this?

Could this really be Joel? The same beautiful baby I had given birth to? The same little boy who had run on the grass, been lifted onto his daddy's shoulders?

My eyes traveled over the arms, the legs, the feet without toes. The right hand had no fingers; the left arm did not even have a hand. The head, burned deeply down to the skull, was surrounded with bandages. I actually had the thought, *Maybe this isn't Joel after all. What if he accidently was switched when he was admitted with one of the other children? What if this is really someone else's child?* It was the same fear new mothers have when they see their newborn child for the first time in the hospital nursery.

Joel hit the bath water with his arms, experiencing the new sensation of water on grafted skin. At first he screamed, but then his arms started whirling about and up splashed the water with each smack of the arms. His eyes twinkled. He was smiling. This *was* Joel, our son, so excited about the water, having fun.

We began to play together with the water. I found a boat on the edge of the tub and pushed it at Joel. He pushed it back, giggling. I pushed it back a second time, harder. He hit it with his arms, sinking it beneath the waves, laughing now, an all-out belly laugh. Yes, this was Joel! He was playing just as he had before the accident. The same Joel was there—inside this new body! I hummed along in my mind the words of the song:

I am a promise.
I am a possibility.
I am a promise
With a capital "P."
I'm a great big bundle of
Potentiality.

Yes, Joel was the same bundle of promise and potential that he had been before the accident.

As Mike and I began to adjust to the new Joel, we realized we were going to have to help Jami cope with this great change also. Mike remembered well Jami's reaction to him when she saw him for the first time after the accident. . . .

Mike was soon to be discharged from the hospital. He looked the best he had since his injury five weeks before. But to Jami, her daddy looked very strange indeed. She backed away from him, scared. Mike was hurt. He ached to wrap his arms around his daughter.

The ice was finally broken when Jami got hold of my wallet. Mike and Jami played "hide mommy's wallet" in the front lobby of the hospital. Playing together brought them closer together. After this game, Jami would sit on Mike's lap, but she didn't like kissing him.

Having experienced Jami's difficulty in coping with a relatively small change in his appearance made Mike aware that we needed to prepare Jami to deal with the great change in Joel's appearance.

Mike and I took Jami into the den of the Norwood home. *She is such a tender spirit,* Mike thought. He wondered how she would react to her "new " brother. I sat beside Jami on the sofa and Mike perched on the arm next to her. We fully expected it would take a lot of explanation to help her understand.

"Because Joel was burned," Mike began, "he no longer looks the same."

"Yes, his skin is redder—it feels and looks different," I added.

"We have these pictures to show you, Jami. If you have any questions, honey, we will try to answer them," Mike ended.

Jami picked up the pictures and stared at them for a long minute. Then she said, "He may be changed on the outside, but he's the same on the inside." She flicked her long, dark eyelashes up and down and looked up at us inquiringly as if to say, "Well, now that we've got this over with is there anything else you would like to say," or "when are you getting to the important stuff?"

She caught us totally off-guard. Our minds had been trying to cover all the possible soul-searching questions she was going to ask—but during this first encounter she never asked them.

The next step was for Jami to be with Joel again in person. I was apprehensive, to say the least.

Upstairs at the hospital I loaded Joel into a wheelchair and we proceeded to the basement of the hospital where we stood guard by the soda and candy machines. We waited.

As Jami and Mike peaked around the corner, they saw a form of a body flooded in a sea of white bandages, blankets, and pillows. Jami's eyes quickly came to rest on the lively brown eyes which seemed to counter the redness of the expressionless face.

Joel's white teeth, which were fully visible because of burn loss and contractures, seemed to smile. Cautiously Jami approached Joel, still focused upon his eyes. Maybe she intuitively knew most of Joel's external appearance had changed except for his eyes.

Jami stopped. As if to size up the situation, she cocked her head sideways and said a sheepishly soft, "Hi, Joel." She then engaged Joel in a series of games. With each game she became more comfortable with him. When their time together was over, Jami hugged her brother, good-by.

*The Race
for
Rehabilitation*

Groundhog Day, 1980, was the day Joel emerged from the hospital to enter the world of home and community. Yes—of all days—Groundhog Day! Our son was coming home! Back to our house, our yard, back to his friends, back to life! I hadn't slept well for nights just anticipating everything that needed to be done so that Joel would have the very best of care.

That morning as we picked him up at the hospital, packed his suitcase of toys, assorted bandages, lotions and medications, our race seemed to be beginning once again. The same thrust needed to run with Joel to the waiting ambulance back on September 15, 1979, was still there. Only this time, we slowly carried him to our car.

His eyes seemed to be taking in everything outside the hospital. Cars and trucks on the street honked at each other; their colors and metallic shine fascinated Joel as he intently watched them from the car window. Mike started our car, and we started cruising down the streets of Boston toward home.

I watched Joel carefully. The fast movement of objects past our car, the buildings, the other vehicles, the people on the street, he seemed to be seeing for the first time. Every honk, every outside sound caught his immediate attention; his little helmeted head quickly turned around in the directions of the noises. But what he failed to notice were the quick glances of surprised passengers in cars that passed us.

Jami was there in the back seat next to Joel, pointing out different colors from her side of the car. She took out books and leafed through them quickly, too quickly for Joel. Jami was so excited! Her brother was finally here beside her, going home! Her four-year-old mind couldn't quite handle what was going on as she excitedly took out toys, books, anything she could get her hands on, to entertain Joel. Their relationship seemed to be starting over in some ways, while in other ways just continuing where they left off.

The week before, Mike and I had discussed what type of homecoming we wanted for Joel. We felt like throwing a gigantic party—a hero's welcome! Mike wanted a line of trumpeters outside the house heralding Joel's arrival. I could see a large banner across the entrance, "WELCOME HOME, JOEL." But we finally decided on a quiet, private homecoming. We didn't even know if Joel remembered what home was like. What does a two-year-old remember about home after being away almost five months? We showed Joel pictures of our home, and he would look at them, but he was not yet highly verbal so had a difficult time ascertaining how much he could comprehend.

As we rolled down the expressway toward New York, I kept thinking about what lay ahead. It *was* a big deal—homecoming. How could we handle everything? Joel's physical care was primary in my thoughts—a very big consideration.

I had contacted friends and students at the college where Mike taught. This year there seemed to be an abundance of nurses whose husbands were attending graduate or undergraduate school. Many were willing to help—and so excited about Joel. At first I had mixed feelings about so many people helping out with Joel's physical care, but Mike wisely discerned that it would be enough for me just to handle running the totality of the family operation— the house and the activities and people. If others could adequately care for Joel's physical needs, which were great, we should let them, he said.

Scheduling of the five nurses, including myself, was on my mind. These nurses would change Joel's head dressings twice or more a day. His dressings covered his severely burned, open skull. During these dressing changes it was also necessary to unbandage his arms and legs, to inspect his newly grafted, tender skin for areas that had open sores developing or needed special attention, to apply emollient cream, and to rebandage them. Splints must be applied to his arms during the days and also to his legs at night. Eyedrops were needed four times a day to moisten his eyes. The nurses would have to work on a regular routine basis, for it would be impossible for us to make up a different schedule every week.

The next big thing on my mind was the surgical supplies we would need—these alone were overwhelming: sterile and nonsterile gloves, ace bandages, safety pins, splints, gauze bandages of many different sizes, emollient creams, sterile salt water for Joel's head dressing, peroxide, silver nitrate, medicines, and tapes. How in the world were we going to shop and pay for all of these supplies? How were we going to store them?

Joel couldn't really walk yet by himself. He would take a couple steps with great urging if we would hold onto his hand. How could I keep Joel entertained sitting in one place all day long? What were the days ahead going to be like?

In one sense, we were bringing home a two-year-old, but in reality it seemed like we were bringing home a six-month-old baby. As I thought on all these problems, it seemed as though we were preparing our home as a live-in hospital. We had to care for Joel as though he were a patient. But he was also our son. And the rest of us were living there, too, and it was important that all of our needs be met. How was I going to prepare meals? Shop? Do laundry? Answer the phone? Clean? Plus everything else? How were we going to carry on with normal living?

One great challenge had been met: Joel had survived one of the severest burn injuries ever. But now we faced an equally great challenge: what kind of a life would he lead? How could we aid in the total rehabilitation of our son? How could we maximize Joel's productivity as an individual in society, as a contributing member? How could we restore our son's joy for living after all that he had lost? And at the same time, how could we survive as a family unit with family goals and individual goals?

We drove into our driveway. The moment the car stopped, Mike ran into the house with Joel in his arms. He carried him throughout the house, showing him all the rooms. This was the moment we had been waiting for, for so long. All the pain, suffering, displacement in Boston was for this—to bring Joel home. To bring all of us home—together—under one roof, in our home. To return to normal living as a family.

In some ways, it was like starting over again with everything in place. The house was immaculately cleaned. The children's toys had been washed. The mail was stacked up on the kitchen counter. The refrigerator was well-stocked. Our supper was delivered to our door that evening—hot and delicious.

But all Mike and I could think of was getting through the next couple of days, trying to figure out what the routine would be.

Mike's expertise was organization; he came up with the best ideas for operating efficiently and economically. We started to train the nurses right away. We made a list of all the specific treatments needed on Joel. When the nurses finished with their tasks, they charted their treatments and observations in a notebook we kept in Joel's closet along with all the supplies.

The phone started ringing. It seemed we were always answering it to hear someone say, "Welcome home."

"Jan." It was Else. "I want to bring over one of my down-pat dinners. You can have your choice of chicken in cream sauce or a fantastic lasagne. Which one would you like me to make you?"

I couldn't believe this! People actually were calling to ask us what we wanted them to fix for us as if we were in a gourmet restaurant! As if it was their privilege to serve us! Mike and I each gained ten pounds over the next weeks.

The doorbell was always ringing, too. After awhile we just instructed the people who came regularly, "Walk in, please. Then we don't have to answer the door." If we were eating supper and the doorbell rang, we'd just shout, "Come on in." This seems rather rude, but it was the only way we could feel undisturbed and continue to function without interruption.

We scheduled the nurses to arrive promptly at the same time every morning. That way we could at least start the day off in some organized fashion.

Most mornings I thought I would die. I was so tired I didn't think I could make it through the next hour, let alone the whole day. Joel was usually up at least four to six times a night. We didn't know if he was having dreams or if he was just uncomfortable, but he would wake up screaming and kicking the rails of his crib with his splints.

Soon, Christian friends started asking, "How was your night last night? We have been praying specifically that you will get rest." Sometimes their questions scared me because I had to answer, "You know, I don't even remember what last night was like." I was just *so* tired.

But tired or not, during the days we concentrated on strengthening Joel. He needed a high-protein diet to replenish the muscles he had left so that he could be stronger. He needed to gain weight; he needed vitamins and calories. I put supplements in his bottles of milk so that he would ingest even more calories and more protein. We kept a record of everything he ate to insure he was eating enough.

With eating came the problem of getting the food in Joel's mouth. The scars in his cheeks and on his jawline were so deep and heavy that his jaw could barely open. So we had to flatten the food for him. Even if we tried to place an M&M in his mouth, we had to squash it to fit it in. We had to cut everything up in little pieces, then push it up and back into his mouth. Without fingers, and minus one hand, he couldn't possibly feed himself yet, particularly when a spoon wouldn't even fit in his mouth. Many of our mealtimes revolved around Joel for one hour.

Soon we were able to contact a physical therapist who was willing to come into our home to help Joel exercise and learn to walk again. It was important for this woman to come into our home so that we wouldn't have to expend our energy and time going out for therapy.

Joel's first reaction to all these people who worked with him was to scream. It took him a good month to stop screaming at each person who worked with him, both the nurses and the physical therapist. His screaming was intense and would sometimes continue during the entire dressing change. He screamed as soon as he saw the nurse come. He screamed when the nurse unwrapped his ace bandages. He screamed when the physical therapist entered the house and all during the therapy. And he screamed at night. This created even more tension in an already tense situation. We thought we were losing our minds!

Mike went back to work, but he couldn't believe how exhausted he was. He could barely stand up for an hour's lecture without feeling physically drained. He wasn't used to being so tired all the time—frustrating to a man who always had extra energy. He was frustrated at his fatigue also because he was eager to help out at home. He knew he was desperately needed.

The correspondence we received was phenomenal. Cards, letters, phone calls. The volume got so heavy that we decided to send out a newsletter to keep concerned people up to date with what was happening with Joel and our family. In return, these people continued to write us of their love and concern. Above all, their prayers kept us going, kept us running. During the difficult nights sometimes, when I thought I was losing my mind, I thought, *Well maybe somebody out there is up right now and praying for me right now as I'm in semi-delirium.* It was something to hold on to.

When people said to me, "Jan, it must be awful for you." I just stared at them. I could not give in to how tired, discouraged, and frustrated I was. I did not need to hear how awful it must be. I was living it. Every day. When someone talked about our tragedy as just that—I couldn't handle it. If I thought about it, I would not be able to get through the day. I had to concentrate on the positives, such as, *Joel did this for the first time today. He actually walked across the room by himself.* Or, *Joel got up to 1800 calories today.*

I could not dwell on the negatives; there were too many. So when someone said, "Jan, I don't know of anyone who could do a better job at this than you," I was encouraged. Or, "You guys are doing something I could never do," kept us going. "Keep up the good work—we're praying for you all the way!" was a booster. It was people who could do nothing but dwell on the tragedy who dragged us down during the early days.

The network of concern did not stop with Joel's homecoming. Many people were running with the Sonnenbergs in the race for rehabilitation.

Vicki Paul, was one of the special helpers in the early days. She washed dishes, did laundry, cleaned the house, freeing Jan to devote her energies to Joel's care.

Jan's friend Barb arranged for meals to be brought in for the first two months. Many people had volunteered to provide food, and Barb organized the menu to avoid having lasagne ten nights in a row, or two weeks of meat loaf, or a month of tuna casseroles. Volunteers let her know what specific foods they could make, and she scheduled their offerings to provide a varied menu: chicken with swiss cheese and broccoli spears, pot roast, stews, salads, fruit, homemade bread.

Members of local congregations wanted to help, and there was a special way they could do so. Joel needed to have 100% cotton clothes; these would allow his newly grafted skin to breathe better and cause less itching than other fibers. Cotton clothing was difficult to find in a polyester society in the dead of winter, and Mike and Jan didn't have the time or energy to shop. So people brought and made clothing for Joel—overall outfits, pagamas, shirts. One woman made T-shirts with velcro fastenings in the back to solve the problem of getting T-shirts on over Joel's bandaged head.

Giving came in practical, thoughtful forms. The wife of the college president dropped off fresh flowers some days to cheer up the family. Another friend called and asked if she could clean their house for two weeks since an opening had occurred in her own schedule and she wanted to help. Another woman, aware of the volume of correspondence, offered to give secretarial help. A professor colleague of Mike's asked if he could read to Joel once a week for thirty minutes. One woman baked Joel's favorite dessert, brownies, twice a week and drove twenty minutes each way from her home to deliver them.

Jami was a part of our total, vigorous effort to restore Joel to as normal a life as possible. We were all learning how to care for Joel together. But it was hard for Jami to have a different brother than the one she had known. She wanted Joel to go outside and play with her. We tried to explain that for right now we were trying to help Joel be as much the same as possible and that though he would never look the same until he got to heaven, he might be able to walk as he had before and that they could have a happy time together. But Joel didn't even play the same as before. We explained that Joel didn't have fingers and that we would have to teach Joel to pick up objects with his wrists.

Right away, Jami started to explain to Joel how to pick things up, showing him by doing it that way herself, this was her way of reaching out to her little brother, the brother who had been her best friend, the brother she had held hands with and protected in her four-year-old way, the brother she had fought with.

"See, Joel, do it *this* way," I could hear her say—encouraging him, teaching, mothering, the way big sisters do. Jami, along with the rest of us, was channeling much of her energy into Joel, into caring and loving him.

She would play with him during his dressing changes, trying to distract him from screaming and fighting. She watched us bandage his arms, his legs, his skull. This tender, sensitive child was seeing a terrible injury few adults could bear to look at.

I remember Jami angry. "I hate Joel." I remember Jami hurting, crying, "Why, mom, why? Why did Joel have to be burned? I don't want Joel for a brother. I don't want a burned brother." Resentment and anger were there, but her caring was there more often.

A good example of this came when Jami brought home a little notebook from nursery school. It was a notebook about our family. She had worked on it for weeks, and her teacher explained how Jami had invested so much time and thought into her project. The book was a collection of pictures she had cut out of magazines and stories she had made up about the pictures.

When I read through the booklet, I was particularly touched when I came to one pink construction-paper page entitled "Joel": on it she had pasted a picture of a beautiful blond-haired boy. A plump, happy child with soft, kissable cheeks.

This is my brother Joel.
Joel crawls and walks. He walks most.
Joel climbs, but not today, he can't.
He gives me hugs. He doesn't look like this now. But he used to.
He kisses me. He has a hurt arm.
Sometimes a lady comes over to help Joel walk and he walks all
    over the house.
When I was little I slept in a crib.
I played with my Joel.
My mommy dressed me. But now I am big.
I drink water all by myself. I wash the dishes.
I put my clothes on. I climb trees all by myself.
I help take care of Joel.

One evening while Jami and I were talking at bedtime, she asked, "Mommy, if our house is on fire and we are trapped upstairs, how do we get out?"

"Down the escape ladders right under your bed."

"Mommy, who goes down the ladder first, me or Joel?"

"You, sweetheart, you're the oldest."

"If we are downstairs and trapped in one room and can't get out the door—what happens?"

"We break a window."

"Mommy—let's make sure the child-finders are on the windows so that the fireman knows where me and Joel are. . . . Mommy, I wish Joel weren't burned, I wish he weren't burned."

Jami has probably had the hardest race of all—our beautiful ballerina, tall, dark, thin, graceful. Caring.

You don't see Jami's scars.

You notice her brother first. Joel's scars, highly visible, grab your attention immediately.

But Jami's scars are on the inside.

They run as deep as Joel's scars, not always obvious, but deep; and they hurt.

Jami saw the fire. She saw Joel charred and still smoking. She remembers—the blackness, the smoke, and the terror.

Some of Jami's scars are inflicted by people who don't understand that she's important too.

People who don't understand this brave little runner who has sacrificed for her little brother, who has been without mommy and daddy many times because of him.

Who has

encouraged her brother to run faster when he could barely
run at all . . .

screamed in terror to warn us of his falls outside while
playing . . .

caught his thrusting fingerless hand before crossing the
street . . .

gently guiding

running alongside

pushing him on.

Jami is wounded every time she and Joel are together walking down a street or in a crowd. Some people say, "Hi, Joel. How ya doing, buddy?" They seem to thrive on *his* answer, his response. They don't see Jami there, right beside him, her hurting eyes saying, *Will you notice me, too?*

Jami, in her girlish, childish shyness, bounce, and tender feelings must run very hard in a race she has not chosen. A race that at a very young age she has been forced to run.

She receives little glory for all her efforts, little praise from the sidelines, little reward.

Yet, she must give her best effort just to survive.

The Race
for
Social Acceptance

Joel's physical needs were being cared for as well as possible. The physical therapy was progressing; the therapist was no longer coming every day but just three times a week. Joel was walking by himself. Joel was eating like a horse. Joel had playtime by himself, with his sister, and with all of us as a family. But it was time for us to reacquaint Joel with the world outside our home.

First, Mike took Joel with him on hikes just as he had promised to do on the tape he had made two days after Joel was burned. With Joel on his shoulders, Mike traipsed all over the small college campus where he taught, just as he had done in the past. Mike was so proud of his son. Here was *his* son, out of the hospital, dangling his bandaged, overall-covered legs over Mike's shoulders. Mike wanted to shout to everyone passing by, "Here's my son— look, he's doing the same things as before!" Students smiled, waved, said an excited "Hello" or "Hi" to Joel.

But there were other comments to Mike later. "It seemed you were trying to carry him around for shock value to everyone."

Mike never thought about the shock people might feel at seeing Joel for the first time on these hikes. He was filled only with his own emotions of thankfulness and pride that his son was alive.

On one of these hikes Mike and Joel passed the home of one of Joel's best friends. At least as "best" a friend as a two-year-old can have. Joel and John had played together since they both were sitting up at six months of age. For almost two years they had played together in their sandboxes, swum together in their plastic swimming pools. They had played with each other's toys. Now as Joel and Mike approached his home, John was outside playing on the front porch. As Joel and Mike came closer, John started staring. His mother, Bev, had shown John pictures of Joel, but the closer Mike came with Joel, the harder John stared. When Mike and Joel got very close, John ran into the house.

Even older children had a difficult time—for example, Barb's children, who had known Joel well. Her son Johnny, eight years old, walked by our house after school one day when Joel was on the front porch watching everyone go by. Johnny saw Joel there on the porch from a distance, but when he walked by the house, he couldn't even look up. He just kept on walking, his face cast down, his eyes on the ground.

Johnny's older brother, Bobby, a sensitive boy of ten, had shouted, "I hate New Hampshire, I hate New Hampshire," upon hearing of our accident. He was eager to meet Joel again, and quickly befriended him.

"Mom, I've been thinking about Joel," Bobby stated to Barb one evening. "He's really going to need someone to be his big brother, to look out for him. I'd like to be his big brother, mom. Do you think I could?"

Happy welcome to you,
Happy welcome to you.
Happy welcome, dear Joel,
Happy welcome to you.

It was the two-and-three-year-olds' class at our church during Sunday school time. Palm Sunday, 1980. Joel's first Sunday back in church. Back among so many, many people who had prayed for him, loved him, cared for him and our family.

Joel was scared, so we stayed with him through the class. The children were wonderful. Most of them had heard "Joel . . . Joel" for many weeks. The week before this, we had given the teacher a picture of Joel to show the class. But one picture really isn't enough. And it didn't prepare the adults at church, many of whom were torn between love for Joel and their own fear of "How am I going to react once I really see him?"

Many were afraid they would cry. And I did see tears in many eyes. This said many different things. If verbalized, some of them might have been—

"You poor child, I can't imagine what you've been through."

"If this were my son or grandson, I would die."

"I had no idea it was this bad."

Mingled with the sadness were the joyful feelings—

"Joel, we're so glad you're back."

"Joel, you deserve the very best after all you've been through. We want to help give it to you."

"Joel, I hope my children love you and are your friends. It will be their privilege."

Of course, we were mobbed with people. "Hi, Joel. Welcome back"—everyone eager, so eager to see the face of the person prayed and cried for, for so many, many months. When they saw him, they were so shocked, but they tried hard not to show it. *How could a child be burned so badly and live?* many thought.

One little boy, Ryan, had a difficult time adjusting to Joel. Joel and Ryan had been good buddies since their days in the nursery at church, banging each other over the head with rattles every Sunday morning, two little rought-and-tough hulks of boys. Ryan knew that this was supposed to be the Joel he remembered, but it was so awful, and Joel had been so hurt. In Sunday school class, every time he turned around and looked at Joel, he cried. This went on for weeks and weeks. We were concerned for Ryan and told his parents that we were sorry he was having such a difficult time; was there anything we could do to help Ryan? They were getting somewhat annoyed with his behavior because all the other children seemed to accept Joel as part of the group; they didn't know what was wrong with their son.

Finally, it came out. One day Ryan was playing near Joel, when a little miracle occurred. No one knew it had happened—until later. Excited, Ryan ran up to his mother, red hair flying in the wind, "Mom, mom, guess what? I touched Joel, mom! I touched Joel! I touched Joel and I didn't get burned!" To Ryan, Joel had been fire. That's why he was afraid. If he touched Joel, he thought he would get burned as Joel had. From then on Joel and Ryan were friends again.

And then there were the little girls. Hope was particularly tender. She was younger than Joel—very petite, very affectionate, very protective, very motherly. She always wanted to put her arm around Joel. She gave him hugs. She brought him crayons. She pulled out his chair for him so he could sit down better. She brought him extra cookies during juice and cookie time. "I love you, Joel," she would say tenderly.

All of these parents had involved their children in Joel's experience. They explained what had happened. They explained that Joel needed love, that Joel's parents and sister loved him, that Jesus loved Joel, and that they should do the same. There were differing reactions to Joel—but all had the same outcome. Because the parents accepted Joel, so eventually did the children.

Some parents were eager to have their older children involved in helping our family and Joel. One mother called, "Jan, I would really like to send my Debbie over. She wants to play with your children. Maybe this will gave you a break."

Or, "Bobby wants to come over once a week and play with Joel."

Or "Johnny wants to help you clean out the hamster cages."

And, of course, there were those people who didn't want to accept Joel at all. (Who still don't accept him. And don't want to.)

One day I was in our local grocery store, picking up the usual odds and ends. Joel was with me for the first time. He was in the cart, sitting in the seat. I wondered how people who had never seen him before would react. People who knew nothing about our little boy and his race for life.

One frail, elderly white-haired woman, could not contain herself. She put her wrinkle-creased face right into Joel's and said, "You poor dear—you poor little thing—what happened to you?"

I felt sick. Was Joel a "poor dear"? What would he think of himself if everyone told him this?

"He was badly burned," I stated.

"You poor thing" she repeated. I moved the cart away. I felt like shouting: "He is *not* a poor thing! His name is Joel! He is my wonderful son!"

But I had to put myself in their shoes. How would I react if I were in a store and seeing Joel for the first time? My mind would probably spin with the question, "What on earth happened? Was this child born this way?" There must be something terribly wrong.

I would not know that Joel had been burned. But I sure would wonder. And I would probably keep looking, not believing, somehow thinking that if I kept looking, maybe I could figure out what had happened to him. I would probably push away my grocery cart, afraid that my child would be traumatized by what I was seeing, because, frankly, I was traumatized! I would have to catch my breath. "What brave new world is this?" I would ask. "With such people in it as this?" How could a child like this live? Why? My fear, My ignorance, My reluctance to deal with reality would push me to these questions and thoughts.

Home from the grocery store, I went about putting away the groceries. Soon Mike called from his biology lab.

"Honey, I just talked with one of the secretaries upstairs. She was behind you in the line at the grocery store, but you didn't see her. After you left the store, the check-out clerk muttered, 'Why do they bring that child out in public? What a disgrace!'

"The other clerk in the line next to hers replied, 'He's just a child. They can't lock him away in a closet.'

"To which came the reply, 'I just wish they wouldn't bring him in here!' "

We were hurt. Hurt that people didn't (and still don't) understand. Hurt for Joel. Hurt for ourselves as parents. How would these attitudes affect him? How would his personality develop if he heard these things? How would he feel about himself?

I took Joel to the shoe store to get his first pair of shoes since he had been burned. Joel was excited! "Shoes!" he exclaimed.

I walked bravely into the store, determined to be enthusiastic— determined not to show fear at other's reactions.

"Hello," said the salesman as he looked at Joel and gulped.

"Hello," I smiled. "I have a very, very, special little son here who needs a very special pair of shoes."

"Okay," smiled the man, but I could see a little hurt in his eyes.

"Joel was severely burned in a car accident. We're here today

The Race for Social Acceptance   147

to buy him his first pair of shoes since his injury. I just have no idea what size he wears, but I know his feet are very, very wide due to scarring. All of his toes are gone, too, which might present problems in fitting."

I had called the store earlier to tell them I was coming in with my son. Did they have wide shoes? I didn't want the trip to be a waste of time. I told them Joel had been severely burned. But, of course, no one can really be prepared by just words if they have never seen a severely burned person before. No visual picture comes to their mind.

Soon a mother with a son near Joel in age came into the store. She was immaculate, well-dressed with a neat hair style. Her son was beautiful. He, too, needed shoes. He, too, was excited. She sat down near us. Her son stared at Joel. Soon he stopped staring and went over to the fish tank on the other side of the store.

I knew the woman probably wondered what had happened. I decided to be the first to speak. "Joel was burned in a car accident. That's why he looks the way he does." I felt stupid saying this, but I felt forced to explain Joel—somehow needing this woman's positive or empathic response.

Her response? She ignored me. Like I didn't exist. She moved a few chairs further over. She kept watching her son at the fish tank. This was worse than if she had said, "So what?" because at least then I could have yelled something back. Instead, her silence made Joel and I invisible, as if we didn't exist. I felt like I had been cut by a knife.

Then a mother came in with her young daughter. When she saw Joel, she picked up her daughter and walked out of the store. Now I wanted to cry. Joel's happy occasion, his first pair of shoes, had been ruined. And if I was having such a hard time coping with these negative responses, what would it be like for Joel? I could reason, rationalize, but Joel was too young to cope this way. Besides, it was his very person, himself, they were rejecting. At Easter we visited in the home of friends. Easter was a special holiday, usually spent with family; but our extended family—made up of grandparents, aunts, and uncles—lived far away. So we tried to spend the holiday with special friends who might also be in the same predicament. We had finished a delicious, Easter dinner with all the trimmings and were leaning back in our chairs, relaxing. Jami and Joel were playing in the front yard when two children from the neighborhood came over to play.

"You're disgusting," spit one of the children at Joel.

"You're ugly," screamed the other.

Joel cried. Jami came running inside: "Daddy, mommy, some boys are being naughty to Joel!" Our hearts were stabbed.

One week later we were watching a baseball game at the college. Joel and Jami were riding Big Wheels up and down the sidewalk near the baseball diamond. Two children—boys about five years old—caught a glimpse of Joel and ran screaming the other way. I asked myself, *"Will I ever get used to this?*

Later that afternoon I was carrying grocery bags out of our car into the house. As I lifted the last bag into my arms, two children, perhaps eight years of age, came walking along the road outside our home. After watching Joel climb out of our car, one asked the other, "Why does that kid wear a monster mask? Why doesn't he take it off?" I quickly glanced at Joel. He apparently hadn't heard what they said. I was relieved.

But it bothered us. What should we say to these people? Was anger the solution? Intolerance? Bitterness?

We felt an urgent need to communicate with the world about our son. We wanted him treated like a whole human being, with respect and dignity. We did not want Joel to be rejected, to be looked upon with horror, fear, or disgust. We did not want the world to be a fearful place for our son.

The next time I was in the store with Joel, I decided, I had to model for him how he should act toward others. If I saw people staring, I would try to ignore it. If it got offensive, I would say, "Hi—this is Joel. What's your name?" trying to break the barrier of ignorance, trying to say, "Joel is a person, too, just like you."

Sometimes it did break the barrier. Many times they just walked away. But sometimes they smiled, or perhaps talked with us.

Spring, 1980

Spring! Wildflowers. Green grass. Gurgling brooks. Bugs. Worms.

> But they that wait upon the Lord shall renew their strength;
> They shall mount up with wings as eagles;
> They shall run, and not be weary;
> They shall walk and not faint."

The verse, one of my grandmother's favorites, my mother had found in her worn Bible back on September 15, 1979, was still with us. As Joel entered the third spring of his short, but miraculous life it seemed our family was experiencing this strength in a vibrant way.

Each day as I looked out our kitchen window to check on the children, I saw Joel and Jami playing in the sandbox together. Running races, picking flowers. Turning rocks over, checking for worms. Crossing the street together. Chugging up the hill, along a small stream of water, throwing in sticks and stones. Seeing and feeling the splashes. Hearing spring. Spring! The earth was coming back to life! So was Joel. Springing up from devastation to love and life.

Learning to walk had been difficult without toes. Now he was beginning to jog along. Soon he would run! Soon he would climb! What more could Joel do? What were the limits to the rehabilitation of our son? He was playing with his toys. He put puzzles together. He could draw with his wrists together holding a pen. His twinkling eyes looked closely at the wildflowers. He watched birds flying from tree to tree. He was drinking in his world—the world we had wanted him to *live* in.

Mike and I were recharged with the vibrancy of life—of Joel's life. We were recharged to run new, even more challenging races.

Joel was coming back to life, gaining and remastering skills he had lost. But what about Joel's face and hands? Couldn't Joel's face be restored? Couldn't it look better? And what about his hands? Didn't they have bionic hands to give people these days? Joel had lived, hadn't he? The impossible had already happened. Joel was alive and seemed to be coming back into a functional life. Medicine was performing modern-day miracles, wasn't it? We were ready to soar off into the clouds. To mount up with wings as eagles!

But it wasn't the time to soar. Someone had to slow us down to a steady run—maybe even a walk. . . .

As Joel began to have more and more plastic surgeries, we began to wonder if he really was, indeed, getting the best that there was to offer. Couldn't he look better? Were these surgeries the best he could be getting? Basically, we were angry that Joel wasn't looking as good as we thought he could. We decided we needed to confront Joel's plastic surgeon with our feelings. I had wanted to do this before, but I hadn't.

Way back in October, about four weeks after Joel had been hospitalized at the Shriners Burn Institute, I had first met Dr. Donelan, Joel's plastic surgeon.

"Who are you?" came the pointed question from the other side of Joel's plastic unit. It was my voice—not just inquiring, but disgusted, brazen, frustrated, wanting to know who this young doctor was looking in on my son, standing there at the foot of his bed? Who were all these physicians who came by here? Why didn't they notice me? Didn't they know I was Joel's mother, a very important person in his life? Why was he looking in on Joel? Maybe he was from the infectious disease team from the medical center nearby. Maybe he knew something about the temperature fluctuations which had me so worried. Maybe he could give me some insight into what was going on with Joel's physical condition right then.

"Who are *you?*" came the reflected reply, the doctor's eyes intently watching Joel, traveling past the 8″ × 11″ portrait at the foot of Joel's plastic unit, his eyes concentrating from a distance on the small body hidden in bandages, enclosed within a prison of plastic walls.

"I'm Joel's mother," I emphasized, voice icy, disgusted yet imploring, and I wanted to add, "Who else do you think I'd be?" But instead I fired back again, "Who are *you*?" I wasn't going to let this go.

After a quick glance up from the flow chart, came the quiet reply, "I'm a plastic surgeon."

I was startled. An unexpected answer. I had not seen a plastic surgeon by Joel's bed for quite a few weeks now, in fact not since he had been transferred from the other hospital. I wondered what this surgeon intended to do. Operate on Joel? But what procedure?

Instead of asking these questions, I went back to talk with Joel. When I looked up, the surgeon had already left. I was disappointed. There were so many things I wanted to ask, like the loaded question I had launched at the first plastic surgeon I had met, "What can you do for Joel? What can your skill in plastic surgery do for our son?"

I remembered my early days in an undergraduate school of nursing at a major medical center. The chairperson of plastic surgery had come to lecture to us one day, a very informative and captivating presentation as the physician showed slides of what plastic surgery had done for people. Some procedures seemed minor, others major, but all cosmetic with wonderfully beautiful results. None of the slides had shown fire's devastation and scars which could not be erased, let alone made beautiful. None had shown functional plastic surgery—surgery basic to restoring a person as a productive member of society; surgery that had some definite cosmetic effects but which really could never replace that which had been lost.

So now, this spring, I was asking the same question I had asked before during the first week Joel had been hospitalized: "What can your skill do for Joel?" As I said, the question was mixed with anger that Joel didn't look as we expected he should look after several surgeries that had been performed on his eyes and mouth over the last several months.

Dr. Donelan had the unpleasant job of answering the loaded question disguised in a confrontation. I stated rather brazenly, "We really think you are too young to work on our son, that the only person who should work on Joel is someone with at least twenty years of experience." I gulped as I heard myself say this. My heart was beating fast. I felt awful confronting the young surgeon with this statement, but it was the way Mike and I felt. We had to be truthful, didn't we? It seemed something had to change.

Dr. Donelan explained that Joel would always be a "freak." I was stabbed by his statement. My son—a freak, I thought. No! Never! Never! In exasperation, it seemed, he went on to explain, "The work I did on your son's eye was to save his sight—so that he would continue to see. The work I did on your son's mouth was to give him a lower lip so that he could keep food in his mouth."

I started sobbing. What did I do now? I felt backed into a corner. We really had no choice after all. Joel was in the very best place he could be and was being worked on by the very best surgeon he could have. *We* had to change. Our expectations were not realistic. Even the very best could never restore Joel to any normal appearance. He did not have enough unburned skin and tissue left to do purely cosmetic surgery. Our son was burned so deeply that he would always look weird! Modern medicine could save Joel's life, but cosmetically, comparatively little could be done.

Dr. Donelan, you, too, are a runner with us in your own race of endurance. Joel's plastic surgeon—young, good-looking, talented.

Wielding the skillful surgeon's knife of sound judgment, precision, and courage—

You run a tough, determined, highly disciplined race of time and distance.

This is not your only work—this plastic surgery on severely burned children at Shriners Burn Institute in Boston;

You are a highly competent plastic surgeon on staff of a world-renowned medical center.

You work on the beautiful people who desire to stay that way

And those less beautiful who want more.

You are also a professor in your field; teaching, guiding, explaining, directing.

But I suspect that working on children, such as our son, is your most challenging and your most frustrating work.

Time brings even more scars to such burned bodies—they are ugly they immobilize.

You excise, graft, remold, stitch—all to preserve, protect and maximize functional ability.

Time brings changing developmental needs to these children as looks become even more important with adolescence as they are groping for identity.

Time brings angry parents, struggling to care for such a devastating injury to their child as best they can—parents who question, who need and want information, and who sometimes are never satisfied.

Time brings new techniques, newly acquired knowledge which must be tried and taught. There just isn't enough time it seems.

We have seen your high-paced travel down hospital halls, in three-piece suits, all professional.

We have watched you bend over our horribly scarred young son to scrutinize your work on his face—analytical eyes.

You keep your distance as a runner. This hurts us. But you must keep enough space between yourself and the rest of the pack. For if you come too close, the other runners' pain hurts you, drags you down, slows your pace.

I have seen your eyes with tears only once.

That was enough.

I learned something from you.

A sensitive man working on our son, Joel, and his burned friends, is a man in whom we can place our trust, a man whose emotion as well as skill fuels his work.

A man driven toward excellence for Joel as well as himself is indeed, a fine surgeon.

We admire your surgical skill.

We thank you for your work.

In June, 1980, it became clear to us that though Joel was receiving free care at the Shriners Burn Institute, his recurrent hospitalizations would be costly and financially draining. He had only been admitted to the hospital once since his initial discharge, but Mike wisely discerned that over the next years we would need some sort of reliable financial assistance.

Transportation to the Institute was costly if we flew. But the trip by car seemed to be too much of an emotional drain; we were exhausted by the driving and still felt recurrently vulnerable on the highway. What energy we had left after our hectic life needed to be carefully preserved. Traveling by plane seemed to be the least emotionally and physically taxing.

The cost of staying in Boston was also prohibitive. Housing as well as meals were costly. So was city transportation, whether by bus or taxi.

How were we going to manage this constant financial drain? Our son, only two years old, needed to have at least one of his parents in attendance while he was hospitalized having surgery; this seemed the least we could do for him while he was so uncomfortable and in pain. But how were we going to afford these trips?

We sought out possible avenues of help. One was the local chapter of a philanthropic organization. We met with the leader of this group. We brought Joel into his office. We explained our current situation, problems, and financial needs. It was the first time we had asked someone for help. We felt humiliated doing this—asking for money. But it seemed necessary for us to have some assurance of help as we approached the end of the first year since our accident and faced the years ahead.

We were even more humiliated at this man's reply to our request for help. He gruffly retorted, "We don't have that much money to fund you staying with your son in Boston. Why don't you just take him to the hospital and leave him there? What's he doing out of the hospital anyway? And why do you need to travel by plane to Boston? Why don't you just take a train and save money like everybody else?"

He seemed disgusted that we were there. Disgusted at Joel. Upset that we had asked for help.

On the way home in the car, Mike was furious. How dare anyone treat us like that? Treat his wife like that and his dear son? He wanted to turn the car around, march back into the man's office and smack him between the eyes.

I was depressed. I thought over the conversation and didn't see how we could have done anything different to change the man's mind. He clearly seemed to be against us right from the first as though he knew before he even met with us that he didn't really want to help us. *What will happen now?*

Were we really that weird to want to stay with Joel, our two year old son, during his hospitalizations? Should we drive to Boston and leave Joel off at the hospital and drive home?

Back home, the ring of the telephone interrupted these thoughts.

"Hello, Mrs. Sonnenberg, this is Jim Blake. I'm with the Rockland County Volunteer Fire Department. We heard your son has been severely burned and we wondered if there was anything we could do to be of assistance to your family."

"Mr. Blake, I don't believe you called just now." I proceeded to tell him what had happened to us that morning.

"Well, we certainly would be happy to assist you in any way that we could," was his sympathetic response. The New York Rockland County Volunteer Fire Department generously paid for our airfare to Boston and back from that time forward.

We were still receiving a great deal of correspondence from various people all over the United States. Some of the letters would include a check for ten, twenty, or sometimes fifty dollars. But I was not prepared for the contents of one particular letter.

The white envelope I had just taken out of the mailbox had unfamiliar handwriting on the front. The note read, "I have heard of your situation from a friend. I would like to give you this gift to help you at this time." Enclosed was an anonymous cashier's check for $1,000. $1,000! Could all those zeroes be real?

Soon after this our church began giving us money through a fund set up to assist us—the same amount every month so that we could count on it. This was so helpful. It meant that neither Mike nor I needed to go out hunting for an additional part-time job. It represented the love and care of many people who knew that a sum of money was needed, regularly, to supplement our income.

Our little family was exuberantly anticipating the community celebrations of picnics, parades, and fireworks on July 4. Jami's and Joel's eyes gleamed with excitement and anticipation of all the activities as we explained to them about our country's birthday and how many families had to suffer and many people died in order to win our freedom. Freedom to say what we want to say, freedom to go to church anywhere we want, freedom to do what we want to do any time we want to within the law. Our town's Fourth of July Community Picnic and Playday included bike contests, a parachute for the children to stretch out, and a band. There would be many, many people there; we knew only a few of them.

Before we left the house that midday, I whispered nervously to Mike, "Do you really think we should go ahead with this?"

"It's the Fourth of July!" Mike retorted. "It's a fun time. Joel has just as much right to go to this celebration as anyone else. We're going!"

"But Mike, so many people—"

"Honey, Joel has got to get out. If they stare, they stare. Keeping him away from activities isn't good for him. We've got to go out and face the world."

"But, honey, he's so young. What is he going to think of himself?"

"So you want to wait till he's ten years old and then he finds everybody staring at him all of a sudden? This is going to be his life. He's alive in the world and he's got to go out into it. If you want to stay home, fine. But Joel, Jami, and I are going."

We went. As a family. Driving down our mountainside street, I couldn't help but think of Mike's strategy for Joel as being typical of a former football player. He was still ramming the line. With all he had. Head on. Tackling the obstacle. Meeting the problem face to face—muscle to muscle.

I have never played football. I didn't think these tactics were quite what I would do if it were up to me. What would I do? I would probably shelter Joel for a little while longer. Picking experiences carefully for him. Not too much social contact right away with people we didn't know. I'd probably avoid problem situations as much as possible. But was that really good for Joel? Maybe Mike was right. . . .

Well, today we would see if this was the preferred strategy. But I was frightened. "How will so many people react, at one place and at one time, to Joel?" I didn't want anyone to notice me— that I was different. That Joel was different.

How were we going to manage all these people? What would we do if everyone started staring at us. If little children in large numbers came around pointing and laughing at Joel—as if he were in a cage at a circus and they were enjoying the show. What were our options of behavior in this kind of situation?

Well, we certainly could retreat from battle. We could certainly leave the scene and flee home. Or, at the other extreme, we could execute an all-out full-scale attack and announce to the gathered crowd: "Joel has been burned in a car accident. That's why he looks different. He has suffered horribly. He is a child of great courage and love of life. So stop staring."

What if the parents moved their children away from Joel? What if they wouldn't allow their children to play with him? What if they thought he had some contagious disease or something? I would be crushed for Joel. For my little son who needed other children to play with—to love and accept him. But what would Joel think of all this? My two-and-a-half-year-old son? How would his developing self-image absorb these people's reactions to himself? How could he develop the proper amount of self-esteem with everyone goggle-eyed or horrified over him? And what would sensitive Jami think?

As we pulled into the parking lot near the community park, another option came to me: take each individaul situation as it came. One at a time, just as we had so far, slowly and confidently. Just as I had done in the shoe store, just as I had done in the grocery store. Just as Mike had done, carrying Joel all around town and around campus on his shoulders.

162   *Race for Life*

We found a vacant park bench and sat our little family down to wait the activities.

It was a beautiful day. Hot and sultry. Great picnic weather. The shade felt good. Cool. I was concerned that Joel might get too hot. If he was too warm, he started itching. The itching was often intense and didn't stop for a long time. It drove him crazy. Plus his body couldn't cool off well with most of his sweat glands burned away.

"There's some men setting up the bandstand," Mike pointed out. "And over there must be where they're going to sell the food."

Few people were there yet. One family walked by, and their little girl noticed Joel. My heart skipped a beat. The child could only be two or three. She pointed at Joel and stared.

"Say hi, Joel." I looked at Joel. I looked at the little girl. She was cute, dark hair, ponytails. Joel was staring at her. He was silent.

"Hi, how are you?" I asked the little girl. She smiled sheepishly, then ran on to keep up with her parents.

"Joel, she smiled. I think she like you," I reassured him. I gave him a hug. Sometimes I still couldn't believe he was alive. Such a precious boy. Joel kept watching the crowd.

Soon some friends came. It was so good to see someone we knew. They greeted Joel and Jami. They gave Joel extra-special warm attention. Bending down to look into his eyes, they said, "Hi, Joel. So good to see you out here today." Their boys were entering the bike contest and had been up all night decorating their bikes. We followed them to the place where the bikes were going to be paraded along with the village fire trucks and a band. Somehow I felt protected with these friends around, as if it said to the rest of the people, "These folks aren't so weird. Look, they have friends. And their children have friends."

Other people accepting Joel seemed to me to be a demonstration to the world that they could do the same thing.

The bikes were all lined up, decorated with crepe paper and ballons and signs. Mike held Joel in his arms so that he could see better. Jami stood by me, peering around the other people in front of us. Many of the children were boys. Some were only four or five years of age, ready to ride their first two-wheelers around the block in the community parade.

Jami exalted, "Look, mommy, at that pink bike. It's my favorite!"

"Me, too," chimed in Joel.

Joel could have been out there, I thought, *if this accident hadn't happened.* We could have decorated up his little three-wheeled motorcycle. *He'd be out there with all the others,* I thought angrily. I thought to the future, *Will Joel ever ride a bike—a two-wheeler? How can he—with no fingers and only one hand?* Well, Mike certainly would think of something—my creative, imaginative husband with his talent for building things and inventing things. He could invent something to help Joel hold onto the handles of a bike. . . .

As the parents and the crowd started cheering on their favorites in the race of brightly colored bicycles, I thought: *Here in this crowd of many people is a young child, our son. All these people are rooting on their favorites in a bicycle race, oblivious to the fact that very near them is a first-place winner. A winner of one of the most difficult races for survival ever. When these children cross the finish line, their bike contest, their race will be over. But Joel isn't. It has just started. And it seems as though it may never be over.* If only I could stand up and somehow direct this crowd to root and cheer on our son Joel and his special sister, Jami! Would they cheer? Would they accept our son as a child full of life and vigor the same as their children? Would they speed him on in his great race?

Ahead of us were many struggles that would be important for Joel to win, such as riding a bike or playing baseball or soccer. But we were in an even greater race right now—one which challenged people's values about life and about themselves and about their relationship to God. It seemed clear to me in those minutes, watching those young children strain to push pedals harder and further, that we needed to light a new fire. We needed to light a little flame within people to race with us for Joel and for his social acceptance. For a life as near normal as possible. For a life which every child, disabled or not, deserved. For freedom to be all that God wanted Joel to be, all that he could be with the abilities he had left. For all that we as parents wanted for him—to be the very best Joel he could be. But for all this, we would need the help of others.

The bicycle race was over. So was the parade. Joel's eyes had danced and gleamed when he saw the huge fire trucks. Jami was afraid of their sirens and had clung to me tightly.

The crowd dispersed and Mike took Joel to the playground nearby. Jami went off with a friend. I sat and talked with Mary, Jami's nursery school supervisor, who was there with her family. I couldn't help but express my anxiety to her about Joel starting school the coming fall. Would the parents welcome Joel into their children's class? Or would they fear that seeing Joel might traumatize their child for life? How could we help these parents prepare their children for our son?

Mary suggested we write a letter explaining the situation, letter from us, as parents of Joel, to other parents.

I thought about this. If we did it, what would we say? I knew what *I* wanted to say. "Our son will be in you child's class and you better prepare your child to be as sweet and kind to Joel as possible. And we don't think we can take it if you're mean." It seemed I was always defensive in my thoughts toward other parents. I couldn't be like this. I must be accepting of them just as I wanted them to be accepting of Joel. This was something I had to work on. . . .

Soon I went off to search for Mike, Jami, and Joel. Scurrying down the hillside to the playground below, I saw large numbers of children playing on the equipment. Children laughing, yelling, having a wondeful time swinging their bodies on the bars and sliding down the slide. Where was Joel in the middle of this? Soon the little white helmet emerged from one of the "tunnels" of the play equipment. Mike was right behind Joel through the tunnel, urging him on.

I gathered Joel up in my arms. "Good job, Joel." He was having such a good time.

I felt the eyes of many of the children turn toward Joel, staring as they continued to play. The eyes seemed to burrow through me. I felt so helpless for Joel. What could we do to keep eyes from staring? Had they been staring at Joel the entire time Mike and he were here playing? I tried to ignore them. But would they never stop staring?

As we walked away from the play equipment to our car, Mike said, "Honey, I've never come so close to hitting someone between the eyes before." He pounded his palm with his fist. "Do you know what happened back there? One of the boys, I'd say about five or six years old, started to tease Joel and brazenly asserted that Joel could in no way go down the slide.

" 'What's a monkey doing riding down this slide?' he accused. As he kept up the harassment, he kept looking over his shoulder to his teenage brothers who were egging him on. My blood was just boiling. I yelled at the brothers and pointed to the boy, 'Hey! What gives you the right to taunt my son? How would you want me to tease you like that?' Glaring at the boy I fired, 'Get down off this slide and don't you ever do that again.' The little jerk nearly ran down the slide and disappeared with his brothers. I can't believe they were so unkind! How can people be like that? What must their parents be like?"

I gathered our clothes together with mixed emotions. Almost a year ago I had thrown shorts, swimsuits, and jeans into various suitcases with great anticipation of excitement to come. Relaxation. Vacation. But the last time we had headed out—we never reached our destination. What would happen this time? I was scared.

It was only a four-hour trip to Camp-of-the-Woods in Speculator, New York. At least that was what Barb had said. "We leave at 5:00 A.M. Saturday morning, Jan, with a short stop for doughnuts and juice at the first rest area."

Again, we were heading out into the unknown. We had never been to Camp-of-the-Woods before. Barb and her family vacationed there every year for at least one week, maybe two and they seemed to enjoy it immensely.

"The kids love the beach, and the water is so clear and clean," Barb always said. "There is so much to do." I glanced over the brochures she had given me. "Camp of the Woods," they read, "vacation on purpose. Come worship and play together. Experience Christian fellowship."

We sure needed a rest, a vacation, a change of scenery. We were all exhausted, sapped of energy from caring for Joel in every way we could.

There were many uncertainties as we headed out that Saturday morning. A major one was that we were headed into the popular Adirondack Mountains of upstate New York to stay at a Christian camp, but we had no guaranteed lodging! We were going on one of the busiest weeks of the season, without reservations!

I had called Barb's sister, Joanne Purdy, three weeks previously. Her husband, Don, was and still is the assistant administrator at camp. I knew that Joanne had heard all about us from Barb, so I went right to the point. "Joanne, we'd love to come up and have a rest. Is there room for us?"

"We'd love to have you, Jan. Every available inch of space is filled for the week you want, but I know that if you are meant to be here something will open up. We would love to have you and finally meet you."

So we just packed and planned as if we already had reservations.

Another friend arranged for us to stay in his cottage some twenty minutes from the camp until a room opened up.

At Camp-of-the-Woods, the family of God was once more preparing a network to receive the Sonnenbergs. When Gordon Purdy, executive director, first learned that the Sonnenbergs were coming, his camp was filled. Since he didn't have a room, he made one. He provided a special room—his plushest accommodations.

Sunday afternoon, Don Purdy, Gordon's son, addressed the two-hundred staff members, many of them college students, and explained the situation. "We have a family moving into camp for the rest of the week. They have been through a very tragic experience." He told the Sonnenberg's story—the horror of the accident, Joel's burns. and the struggle for recovery.

"These people," he said, "are physically and emotionally exhausted. I want each staff member to go out of his or her way to help these people who have been through such tragedy. I want them to receive the red-carpet treatment. I want their time here to be very special. In the dining hall, in the snack shop, on the beach, and while you are baby-sitting their children, I want every one of you to bend over backwards for these people.

"When they leave camp I truly want them to be emotionally, physically, and spiritually renewed. I want everyone to feel responsible for making this a great week at camp for them."

And they did!

As we lay on the beach during our last day at Camp-of-the-Woods, trying to drink in our last measure of the brilliant blue sky and water, the majesty of the surrounding Adirondack Mountains, I reflected on the week just past.

The first Sunday afternoon we had ventured out to the wide expanse of beach owned by the camp. Some five-hundred other families were also there that week, enjoying family vacationing in the sun, sailing, boating, swimming. So as we made our way to the beach area, the same fears surfaced in my mind. I remembered my first sight of Joel's body in the bathtub at the hospital. These people would soon see this same body on the beach. Bare except for the bright blue swimming trunks which covered most of the area where fire had not touched. What would these people do? What would their children do? Run away? Laugh? Gawk? Would it be another Fourth-of-July experience?

I had been frightened at Joel's appearance when the totality of fire's destruction had been revealed to me. And I was Joel's mother! What would these people do? Scream? Faint?

Jami and Joel quickly scampered onto the beach in their swimsuits to join Barb's children playing in the sand—building castles, digging holes, splashing, running, laughing. Don and Joanne's children quickly joined them. Tracey and Donnie soon made a contest of who could get Joel to laugh the hardest. Who could get Joel to have the most fun? They crashed into the waves of the lake, time after time, as Joel would give pretend punches for "knock-outs."

Since that afternoon, our family had been floating around on a cloud of love and care from everyone at Camp-of-the-Woods—for the entire week. The wonderful part was that we didn't have to go around explaining ourselves or Joel to anyone. No one asked us, "What happened to your son?" Word had obviously quickly spread among the families that Joel had been burned in a car accident. Soon people passing us on the sidewalks, paths, and roads were purposely greeting, "Hi, Joel—how are you?" Or, "Joel, my name is . . . I think you're special." It seemed everyone wanted to meet such a courageous little boy whom God would not allow to be totally destroyed by the consuming fire.

It seemed as though we rode through the spacious and beautifully scenic grounds in a limousine. The top was rolled down on the limousine and Joel was standing up and waving to the crowds.

They were waving and cheering him on—totally in love and captured by a little boy and his great race for a full life.

At Camp-of-the-Woods, Joel finally got his hero's welcome.

Don Purdy took us for mototboat rides, allowing Joel to "drive" the boats. He also let Joel "drive" his souped-up Jeep. We went sailing on large sailboats. Mike and I went water-skiing. And at night after children were sleeping, baby-sitters were provided so the two of us could get away to some of the evening events or to restaurants nearby.

During our last evening meal at camp, the table where we were sitting was suddenly surrounded by staff members with trumpets and trombones. The air was charged with excitement. As they began playing, everyone in the dining hall started clapping to the music—adults and children of all ages. Mike hoisted Joel onto his shoulders and bobbed up and down to the music's rhythm. The brass and voices echoed out over the checkered tablecloths, and the wooden floors, the strong smell of coffee and dessert.

> For he's a jolly good fellow
> For he's a jolly good fellow
> For he's a jolly good fellow
> Nobody can deny.

Barb and John, sitting next to us, were crying. People at the tables across from ours were crying. Moved with excitement and charged with exhilarating acceptance for a little boy whom fire had not totally destroyed, because he was still the same little boy of potential and promise.

Joel's eyes were twinkling; his stiff mouth was trying to spread into a grin. His arms, wrapped in ace bandages, stiffly raised up and down to the music as if he were an airplane. I could barely make out his giggles and belly laughs above the roar of the instruments and participating crowd.

Truly, it had been a week of vacation on purpose!

Michael Saraceni

Where are you? We've lost touch with you.

You took action while others took photographs.

You helped pull the pin on the fire extinguisher to stop the flames engulfing our car.

You squirted foam on the car.

Then you heard a cry—

A BABY—IN THE CAR!

That's all you needed. You love children.

You pulled our son out of the car.

Your fingers grabbed onto a half-melted, molten-hot infant seat.

"I saved your baby," you implored, throwing the red-hot infant seat onto the ground, your hands burned.

I hated you in that moment. My baby saved? From what? Death? Certainly only seconds to go for that peaceful finale.

You told us you had had a rough childhood, that you never finished high school.

But you love children.

You called the hospital every day. "How is Joel Sonnenberg?" Sometimes they said, "We are not allowed to give out that information." In other words, "It's none of your business." Other times they said, "He's still critical." So little information.

You visited Joel in January—four months after your demonstration of bravery. You gave him a giant teddy bear as a present.

It sits now in the front foyer of our home. Everyone who comes in our home sees it straight ahead as they walk in the door.

It reminds us of you—

Your act of courage,

Your love of children.

Thank you is not enough—

    for our son's life.

The Race
Toward
Triumph

Today we are well into the longest and possibly the hardest stretch of our race for life, the long-distance endurance run of recurrent hospitalization and rehabilitation. This course takes Joel in and out of the operating room as surgeons work to do the best they can for him, promoting functional ability so he can see, eat, move his legs, arms and neck, and manipulate objects to the highest degree possible.

Someday the final goal will be reached and Joel's race toward triumph will be over. The tape at the finish line will be broken and a large, bold banner, will welcome the runner to heaven's gate: "WELCOME HOME, JOEL . . . WELL DONE." Jesus will keep His promise to Joel, and He will welcome him to eternal life with a body completely restored. Until then, however, we must keep running. We are still running a race of survival through suffering. We must make Joel's "now" as full and productive as it can be.

Four-thirty A.M. the alarm buzzes.

"Joel, it's time to wake up, sweetheart. Today's the day you fly with daddy on the airplane."

Slowly Joel awakens as I carry him downstairs to fill up on his daily morning ritual—two bowls of cereal, juice, toast. I hug him and give him many kisses—something I don't do with such abundance every morning, but today is different. Today Joel and Mike will journey to Boston so that Joel can have plastic surgery early tomorrow morning.

About two weeks before Joel leaves for Boston we start preparing him for the trip and the hospitalization. We talk about it as if it is a natural part of life now . . . and won't it be fun to ride in the plane? We talk about what specific work will be done . . . his mouth will be widened so that his teeth will show and he can fit a whole spoon inside . . . a bone graft so that he will have a thumb . . . nose work so that he will have a new nose.

"Joel, you will have such good times with daddy. He'll build you towers and carry you around on his shoulders and buy you candy bars." I say this with bounce and enthusiasm I don't really feel.

"Joel, do you think your favorite nurses will still be there? I bet so. . . ."

I know that during the day his time will be filled with many activities, everything from physical therapy to many hours of play therapy and recreational therapy. It's the nights that bother me the most. What happens when Joel wakes up in the middle of the night crying and mommy isn't there? This worries me greatly.

"Joel, do you ever wake up in the middle of the night in the hospital?"

He nods his head, "Yes."

"What do you do then, honey? Do you cry? Why do you wake up?"

"Cause it's so noisy—too much noise."

"Well, what do you do then? Do you tell them to be quiet?"

"No, I just sit there."

"Will you tell them to be quiet? Do it for mommy. Do you go back to sleep?"

"Sometimes."

At least his blanket and his stuffed dog, Fluffy, can stay with him, even though mommy can't.

"Joel, I want you to remember something, and this is so very important. Jesus is always with you. Always. He is with you just like Fluffy is. Right there beside you. He is very strong—even stronger than daddy. He knows what is best and He always will be with you. Your guardian angel is right there beside you—just like mommy is right now. He lies down when you're sleeping— right next to you with his arm around you just like mommy is doing right now. Even though you don't see him—he's there. And when it's noisy, maybe he'll even fly over and tell the nurses to be quiet or even maybe try to quiet down one of the kids that might be crying. Just remember that when mommy or daddy can't be there, that's when your angel does double duty—he works the hardest for you then. In fact, your angel deserves to be a five-star general!"

We help Joel get dressed in his best clothes for the plane ride with Mike.

"Joel, you look so sharp!" I say with a lump in my throat as I see him bashfully swell with pride at how nice his clothes look. He does look sharp to me. Not ugly. He seems so beautiful sometimes, so handsome standing there in clothes that a year before I thought he would never wear. Hastily we look over his suitcase to make sure everything is there—pants, tops, Matchbox cars, Fluffy, his picture Bible. Yes, everything is ready. The ache begins. . . .

They're gone. Gone. Silence. It's quiet—so quiet at 6:00 A.M. Jami isn't awake yet and I'm alone to hurt and cry. I like to be alone to cry. I can really let it all out then. I go into the kitchen, pour another cup of coffee, and sit down at the table. Crumbs of toast are still at Joel's place. His bib still has huge globs of food and crumbs on it, and the bowl of milk still sits there—in some strange way these remains of his hurried breakfast seem to be all that is left of Joel in our home.

"No operation," Joel moaned this morning during his meal. I gulped a "I know it hurts, honey, but daddy will be there when you wake up. Don't forget you'll have special treats on the plane too. There will be a surprise in daddy's pocket." And I remember the extra kisses I asked for—for Jami. He walked out the door with Mike. Then he runs back with an extra bear hug, "I love you, mommy. I miss you."

Yes, in the coming years there will be many trips to Boston, much for us to endure with Joel. One important sequence of operations for Joel was the series of surgeries that gave him a thumb to enable him to pick up small objects—a raisin, a crayon. Such a simple action which most of us take for granted, but for Joel, that one thumb was nine months in the making.

After the final operation, a bone graft, Joel wore a huge cast extending up to his shoulder on his right arm. All of us were so excited about seeing Joel's new thumb, about finally reaching the culmination of so many, many weeks and months of waiting, of weeks and weeks in the hospital. Of looking at Joel's cast, wondering at what it contained.

As the Easter season of 1981 approached, Joel's cast seemed like a giant malformed Easter egg just waiting to be cracked open.

We waited in anxious anticipation. We wondered if Joel had any idea of what was happening. Did he have any idea of the significance of what would be unveiled in Boston? His thumb. The only one. The only finger he would ever have. What did Joel understand of this?

During the middle of Easter week, we talked more intensively about what was going to happen. Joel sat on our eouch as we had family time before bed. We talked about the next day: It was an important day. We were again going to Boston. Joel would have his cast taken off. He would see his new thumb for the first time. This would probably be the only finger he ever had in this life. We all were excited!

"Joel, I hear something," exclaimed Mike. "A little voice is coming from inside your cast."

Joel replied, "My thumb! It says get me out of here quickly!"

We started talking about his hand. "Tomorrow you'll see your thumb!"

"FINGERS!" blurted Joel.

"Finger," we stated.

"Five fingers!" retorted Joel.

"No—one, son," Mike stated quietly and slowly.

"Not five fingers?" Joel wondered.

"Joel, you are going to have a thumb and it's going to be the neatest thumb. It's going to help you pick things up and do more things." I tried to reassure him.

"Not five fingers?" Joel questioned again. "Me want five fingers," he cried over and over. Both Mike and I looked at each other, aching for our son. All of us were crying. Mike, choking back tears, hugging Joel to his chest, in a quiet controlled voice explained,

"Joel, you will have five fingers in heaven someday. Someday you will have them, son. Jesus promised."

Epilogue

What you have just read is only a small segment of the total story of Joel's race for life. I don't believe we could ever describe to you the complete horror of Joel's experience or all of our suffering as a family. However, I hope I have sufficiently conveyed to you that despite seemingly impossible odds, our son has survived with all his intelligence, personality, and senses intact. Underneath all the scars and disfigurements he is still the same Joel.

Though this is a story of tragedy and ugliness, it is also a story of beauty and promise. While the scars you have read of and looked at cannot be erased in this life, maximum potential can be found in the power and love of Jesus Christ.

We all bear scars of some kind, don't we? Most of us manage to hide them beneath a normal appearance, but the scars are there. Scars of hurt, pain, anger, despair, loss, hatred; we allow them to sap our energy and wound us, robbing us of our potential and promise that we can be all God intends for a complete and useful life. With His love and power, God can maximize functioning despite these scars—just as He is doing with Joel's and with our family's.

This is also a story about the work of Jesus Christ through His church, scattered around the world, and how through that body of believers of many different denominations, we as a family have been rehabilitated from the wounds of hurt, separation, and loss. It is a story of how the church has run with us. It has been and must continue to be a race with encouragement.

If you have been touched by our son and his race for life, we hope you too, will want to join us. We need you.

As we wrote to the parents of Joel's nursery-school classmates in the fall of 1980:

> Now, Joel's needs are similar to other children's needs. It is important for him to play together with other children, to sharpen his social skills and begin his life as a vital and contributing member of our community. Just as you and your child need love and acceptance from others to maintain your self-worth, so does Joel.

We must prepare Joel's world for Joel, but we can't do it without you.

We are now crossing the threshold of a new frontier. Technological advances in burn medicine have now reached the point of creating a new era: children and adults are walking our streets and living among us who appear to be "aliens." They look different. They have survived extensive facial and body burns, some as much as 70 to 95 percent of their bodies. At a superficial glance, some of these children and adults don't even appear to be human. They seem to be from another planet. But—they are human. They have feelings—love, joy, pain. *They are more normal than they are different.*

As Joel's parents, we have introduced you to what some have described as "the last frontier of the handicapped"—the frontier of facial and body disfigurement. This handicap is unique because it does not rest with individuals afflicted with it as much as it rests on those who come in contact with them. The real handicap of disfigurement lies with society's inability to adequately deal with it, be exposed to it, and wrestle with and change life values traditionally linked with beauty.

Joel lives in a world that for the most part does not want to accept him, or others like him. He lives in a world that sees only the superficial, a world that worships "beauty" and "glamor." He lives in a world that shuns the abnormal, the unusual, the strange, the unexplainable.

We hope that by learning about Joel you will view Joel—and other children like him—as a bundle of potential and promise just as we do, and that you will accept him as a contributing and vital member of our world.

A special thank you to the staff of the Shriners Burn Institute, Boston Unit, who individually run their own professional race, and who also run as a team, racing for the lives of burned children.

Joel was two months shy of his second birthday when the gasoline-fed fire enveloped his father's '73 Chevrolet and burned him while he sat strapped in a car seat designed to protect children from the jolt of a crash.

Jacqueline R. Bruskin of Mount Vernon, N.Y. saw some of what happened that day as she drove through the Interstate 95 toll plaza at Hampton.

"I was pulling out of the right most toll booth and I saw one car pull in behind me," Bruskin told police. "Then I saw, in the rear view mirror, the truck approaching. It didn't seem to be slowing down. The car behind was hit and rammed into me and burst into flames. The truck didn't seem to stop for what seemed quite a long time."

The seven-vehicle collision happened Sept. 15, 1979, almost three years ago . . . .

The insurance game makes you shudder when you realize what the Sonnenbergs have been through and what faces them in the years ahead.

"From September through December of 1979," [their lawyer] said in papers filed with the court, "infant plaintiff, Joel Sonnenberg, underwent at least 10 operations for the express purpose of covering him with his own skin resulting in pain and suffering, mental anxiety and various medical setbacks. Infant plaintiff has since undergone an additional 20 or more reconstructive surgical procedures . . . and it is anticipated that numerous additional . . . surgery can be attempted." [To date, Joel's surgeries number over 30.]

Joel's medical bills during the next 20 years have been estimated at more than $840,000. Reconstructive surgery, doctors have done to date, is valued at $172,200, but Shriners' Hospital for Crippled Children in Boston has not sent the Sonnenbergs any bills.

"It has been tragic, but I've never seen a family that has worked so closely and with such faith," [their lawyer] said of the Sonnenbergs . . . .

The Sonnenbergs' story brings home how dangerous it is out there—on the highways—and how inadequate insurance can be to compensate for the danger inherent in driving.

Last year, Congress tried improving the situation a bit by setting minimum levels of financial responsibility for truckers. There are exceptions, but in general trucks carrying non-hazardous materials interstate must now carry $500,000 in insurance and that minimum will rise to $750,000 in July 1983.

But, on that Saturday afternoon three years ago when _____ drove north on I-95 at the helm of an 18-wheeler, towing a refrigerated trailer loaded with onions, there was little in the government's trucking regulations that required he be well insured . . . .

Among those sharing the road with . . . that day was Michael Sonnenberg, 32, his brother-in-law, Douglas Lynn Rupp, 27, and Joel Sonnenberg, who sat between them in the front seat of what the police report described as Vehicle #5.

Just behind, in Vehicle #4, was Kathleen Rupp, 26, who was three months pregnant; her sister, Janet Sonnenberg, 29, and daughter, Jami Sonnenberg, 3 . . . .

The truck—Vehicle #1 in the state police accident report—approached the toll plaza and collided with one car, sending that car careening to the left, into a van.

"Vehicle #1 then struck Vehicle #3, Vehicle #4, #5, and #6," the police report said.

"As a result of the collision, Vehicle #4 and #5 became engulfed with fire, the result of which came from a ruptured gas tank on Vehicle #5 . . . . The occupants of Vehicle #5 were not able to escape without injuries."

Michael Sonnenberg and Douglas Rupp, their clothing and hair aflame, stumbled from the car, but Joel burned until Michael Saraceni, 20 . . . who witnessed the crash, reached in and freed the boy from his car seat.

Later [the truck driver] told investigators his brakes failed as he approached the toll plaza.

But . . . an inspector for the federal Department of Transportation, checked the brakes and found them operable. "They could have been better adjusted, but they still were able to stop the truck," [he] said.

When put on a scale, the truck and its cargo weighed in at 81,600 pounds—4,100 pounds over the legal limit for New Hampshire roads.

[The truck driver] was charged with second degree assault—"knowingly or recklessly causing serious bodily injury to another." Second degree assault is a felony that, on conviction, could result in a seven-year prison sentence.

He was held in jail for several days, but then bail was set at $10,000, with $9,000 being personal recognizance bail.

That meant [the driver] had to put up only $1,000 in cash to get out of jail.

His employer . . . [an independent trucker from Nova Scotia] put up the money, [the driver] was released and he returned to Canada.

He has never made good on his promise to return and face the charges against him.

Roger Talbot
Sunday News Staff
Manchester Union
Manchester, N.H.